GLORIOUS
BOARDS

For Cherry, Fran, Jennie & Naomi
The best of dinner club friends

When using kitchen appliances please always follow the
manufacturer's instructions.

HQ
An imprint of HarperCollins*Publishers* Ltd
1 London Bridge Street
London SE1 9GF

www.harpercollins.co.uk

HarperCollins*Publishers*
Macken House
39/40 Mayor Street Upper
Dublin 1
D01 C9W8
Ireland

10 9 8 7 6 5 4 3 2 1

First published in Great Britain by
HQ, an imprint of HarperCollins*Publishers* Ltd 2023

Text copyright © Jassy Davis 2023

Jassy Davis asserts the moral right to be identified as
the author of this work.
A catalogue record for this book is available
from the British Library.

ISBN: 978-0-00-864338-6

MIX
Paper | Supporting
responsible forestry
FSC™ C007454

This book is produced from independently certified FSC™ paper
to ensure responsible forest management.

For more information visit: www.harpercollins.co.uk/green

Printed and bound in India by Replika Press

Designer: Jacqui Caulton
Editorial Director: Caitlin Doyle
Project Editor: Sarah Varrow
Production Controller: Halema Begum

DISCLAIMER
The publisher urges the reader to drink, eat, and
prepare food responsibly. This book features recipes
that include eggs. Ensure eggs are fresh and meet local
food-standard requirements. Consuming raw eggs may
increase the risk of food-borne illnesses. Individuals
who are immunocompromised, pregnant, or elderly
should use caution. Be advised: some recipes include
nuts or other allergens. Recipes featured within are not
categorized as halal or kosher.

GLORIOUS BOARDS

Sensational spreads for every occasion

JASSY DAVIS

Contents

Welcome

Fun, elegant, and abundant, grazing boards are a sure-fire way to turn any gathering into an event. It doesn't matter whether it's a midweek movie night-in with friends, a family birthday party, or even a wedding. Every get-together is made extra special when there's a grazing board for guests to tuck into.

If you've ever admired the grazing boards shared on Instagram and Pinterest you'll find this book an invaluable source of inspiration and knowledge. Packed with grazing board inspo, recipes for homemade dishes that add flair, easy ways to elevate ready-made ingredients, and styling tips that make building your board easy, it's the perfect companion for anyone wanting to build their first grazing board or looking for ideas to take their boards to the next level.

As well as classic sharing boards, this book includes brunch boards, hot chocolate platters, Valentine's Day boards for couples, and veggie and vegan boards. From cheese and charcuterie to chocolate and cookies, there's a board for every taste and occasion, and all of them are camera-ready.

Getting Started

Like all good food trends, grazing boards started life in Australia. A couple planning their wedding wanted an alternative to the standard, boring buffet. They wanted something informal, but also show-stoppingly spectacular. Enter the grazing table.

Laden with beautifully arranged canapés, elegant bowls of fruit, smart finger foods, cheeses, nuts, and charcuterie, their grazing table was an immediate hit. Soon every wedding party wanted one, and there were grazing tables, platters, and boards all over the internet.

These days you can find restaurants all around the world offering grazing plates, while specialist suppliers offering boards, bowls, and cocktail forks have sprung up to help people put together their own Instagram-perfect grazing spreads. It's not hard to understand why they're popular. They look incredible, provide a stunning focus point at parties, and they deliver on flavour while not being that hard to do. The big secret is that grazing boards are simple to style once you have the right equipment and know a few smart tricks.

If you're just starting on your grazing-board journey, then the first thing to do is work out what equipment you need in order to create a charcuterie masterpiece.

PICKING THE PERFECT BOARD

The classic grazing board look is oversized and wooden. You can buy all sorts of specially designed boards in a range of shapes and sizes, but you don't have to invest in fancy boards. A standard chopping board or breadboard will work fine. If you want to create a big grazing board, two or three chopping boards lined up next to each other works perfectly.

Your board doesn't have to be wooden – any flat, food-safe surface will do. Baking trays, enamelware, and serving trays can work really well, and, as a bonus, their shallow sides will help stop food rolling off the board. Marble pastry boards also look beautiful, while slate platters bring an element of brooding drama to the table.

For very large grazing platters, you don't need a board at all. Sanitize a work surface or table, line it with greaseproof paper and you have a huge canvas on which to build your grazing table. If you'd like to build grazing stations around the room, use a couple of sanitized, folding card tables lined with greaseproof paper.

LOOKING AFTER WOODEN BOARDS

Keeping your board clean between feasts is obviously important. Not only is it hygienic, but a well-cared-for board will look beautiful year after year.

Prevention is better than cure, so if you're planning a grazing board that contains foods that are likely to stain (or leave greasy marks), then line your board with greaseproof paper before you start. This is also a good idea if you're lining up several boards to create the illusion of one big platter.

Washing your board up straight away is obviously essential, but whatever you do, don't put your board in the dishwasher. It's too hot and too rough and will warp the board. Using wire scourers will also scratch it. Instead, use a sponge, warm water, and washing-up liquid to gently wash the board all over. Make sure you wash all the sides and edges, so it's evenly cleaned. Only washing one side can cause your board to warp and crack. But don't soak it, as that can also make it crack. (Boards are prima donnas.)

Stubborn-looking stains can be removed by sprinkling coarse sea salt onto your board and using a lemon half to scrub it. Let it sit for half an hour, then rinse off the salt.

After washing, air-dry your board, standing it on one edge so the large sides are exposed. Once it's dry, flip it to make sure the edge the board was standing on dries, too. Leaving one edge wet can also encourage mould and warping.

Once or twice a month, treat your board to an oiling. Don't be tempted to use a vegetable or seed oil from your kitchen – it will go rancid and your board will smell. Instead, use a food-grade mineral oil and lightly coat the board all over, gently rubbing it in. Balance the board on one edge and leave it for 3–4 hours to soak up the oil.

If you want to go the extra mile, you can then polish your board with food-safe beeswax or board butter. Apply a little of the beeswax or butter and rub it in with your hands or a microfibre cloth, making sure to cover all the board. Balance it on one edge again and leave it overnight. In the morning, buff it with a microfibre cloth, then store it somewhere clean and dry.

BOARD ESSENTIALS: BOWLS

After your board, the next most important bit of kit is the bowls. They will normally be the first things you place on your board to create the design, so they'll have a lot of impact on the final look.

A range of sizes adds interest when you're designing your board – a small dipping-sauce bowl full of chutney alongside a ramekin of cocktail onions and a larger bowl of hummus will create a flow of heights and shapes, so don't get too stuck on having a set of matching bowls. If you're creating a really big board or table, don't be afraid to go large with salad and fruit bowls. And while white ceramic does go with everything, if you want to create a pop of colour with a brightly hued bowl, go for it. Not everything has to look like it came out of a Scandinavian farmhouse.

The other type of bowl you'll need is a bowl for food waste. Have some bowls dotted around the room for olive stones, cocktail sticks, pistachio shells, and any other bits left behind after eating. You can have rubbish bowls near your grazing board, but keep them at a respectable distance. Firstly, it spoils the look and secondly, it's not impossible a muddleheaded guest will get confused and start using pre-chewed cocktail sticks to spear their olives. Save their blushes by keeping fresh and used items far apart.

BOARD ESSENTIALS: GLASSWARE

Shot glasses, wine glasses, and jam jars are another fun way of presenting things like seafood or miniature desserts. But make sure you use sturdy glasses that, should they get broken, you won't mourn too much, and ideally use them for items that people can lift off the board and take away; a broken glass on the board means the whole thing has to be cleared, which would be a tragic waste of time, food, and effort.

BOARD ESSENTIALS: CUTLERY

Grazing boards are designed to showcase finger foods, so the majority of your guests will help themselves using their hands. But not everyone wants to get their fingers greasy, and you can't always rely on people washing their hands first. A range of artfully distributed serving utensils can help keep your board – and your guests – clean.

If you haven't already sliced your cheese into portions, add a cheese knife next to each chunk so guests can cut themselves a piece.

For oily foods, like anchovies, or greasy foods, like salami, make sure there are serving tools on the board. Cocktail forks look elegant and are perfect for pickles, salads, and charcuterie, while every bowl of dip benefits from having a small spoon nearby (espresso spoons look particularly cute). Miniature tongs can help people snaffle their perfect slice of bread, while skewers and cocktail sticks are ideal for picking up cubes of cheese and slippery foods, like olives.

BOARD ESSENTIALS: PLATES

Overhead images of grazing boards tend to skip showing the practical accoutrements that make eating from a grazing board possible, but that doesn't mean they aren't there. A stack of plates so your guests can pick their perfect bites and then move away from the table is essential. It stops people hanging over the board like herons at a fishing lake, beadily eyeing the next tasty morsel, and means people can circulate around the room. Even if you're sitting at a table together with the board in the middle, having plates means people can fill them and then sit back to enjoy their food – it is a much more relaxed way to eat.

BOARD ESSENTIALS: TABLE LINENS

Alongside plates, you're going to need something for guests to wipe their fingers on. Cocktail napkins, paper serviettes, and rolls of kitchen towel are all good options, depending on the type of board, the final look, and the budget.

LITTLE EXTRAS

If you're making a large grazing board or offering a range of cheeses, consider adding labels to the board so people know what they're eating. Small bottles of olive oil, vinegar, salad dressing, or hot sauce are nice for guests to add flavour to dishes once they've transferred them to their plate. Pinch pots of salt, pepper, chilli flakes, or spice mixes, like dukkah, are another nice way for guests to add extra flavour to their food.

Perfect Presentation

Get the Look

Whether your charcuterie came from Costco or was imported directly from Italy and France, if your grazing table doesn't have board appeal then it's not going to work. Grazing boards should be beautiful. Otherwise, they end up looking like a fox raided your fridge and forgot to put away the packets.

To create the perfect board you'll have to dig into your artistic side a little, but not as much as you think. The secret to a sophisticated and stylish grazing board lies more in how you prepare and arrange your ingredients than in finding your inner culinary Picasso.

CHARCUTERIE FOLDS, RIBBONS & WRAPS

Half- or quarter-folded hams and salamis create simple architectural shapes that add lines and definition to the creative chaos of your grazing board.

Quarter-folds are perfect for larger slices of ham or salami. Simply fold your slice in half, then in half again to make a triangle. These triangles look good laid in lines or S-curves across your board, with the triangles just overlapping each other. You can use them as a subtle way to divide your boards into sections, like little picket fences.

Half-folds are great for charcuterie slices that are too small to quarter-fold. Simply fold your slice in half to create a half-moon shape. You can arrange these in fans or use them to make lines and S-curves the same way you would arrange quarter-folds.

If you want to give shape to wafer-thin slices of hams like Serrano ham or prosciutto di Parma, turn them into ribbons. Fold each slice in half lengthways to create a long rectangular shape, then gently place it on the board, folding it back and forth to create a ripple effect.

Don't discount simply draping slices of ham on your board, especially very thinly sliced ham. The important thing is to make sure that you separate each slice before you lay it down, so the slices are easy to pick up. You don't want your guests accidentally gathering up the entire pack in one go.

To make ham or salami even easier to pick up, wrap it around chunks of cheese to create roll-ups. Alternatively, fold a slice of ham or salami, then thread 1–2 pieces onto a cocktail stick. Add a mini mozzarella ball, an olive, a cherry tomato, or a chunk of grilled antipasti (like cured artichoke hearts or marinated mushrooms), and you have a dainty-looking charcuterie skewer that's easy to pick up and eat.

HOW TO MAKE A SALAMI ROSE

Meat roses are the iconic breakout stars of the grazing board. They're the sculptural way to serve your charcuterie and, if you make them large enough, they can create focal points on your board. Thinly sliced rounds of meat, such as salami, chorizo, saucission, coppa, or bresaola, are ideal for creating rose petals. If you'd like to use other cuts of meat, such as sliced turkey breast or mortadella, use an 8-cm pastry cutter to cut rounds out of them.

The simplest way to make a meat rose is to lay 3–5 slices of charcuterie in a row on your work surface so they each overlap halfway. Fold the row in half, then roll up until tightly wrapped. It should look like a rose bud. These buds may start to unravel as the night progresses, so, to keep them looking neat, slide them onto cocktail sticks, with sage leaves ether side to mimic foliage.

For a fuller flower, you can shape your rose around a glass; the bigger the glass, the larger the rose. A Champagne flute is a good glass to start with, working up to a wine glass. Start by folding one slice of salami over the rim of the glass, so half the salami is inside the glass and half is outside. Add another slice, making sure you overlap the first slice by half. Keep going until you have covered the rim. You should use around 4–6 slices to make this first layer.

Make a second layer exactly the same way, then add another 4–6 layers, but slowly shift the salami so each layer has more of the salami inside the glass than the layer before. You can store your salami roses on the glasses in your fridge for 4–6 hours. To serve them, place a saucer over the glass, then turn it over, gently twist the glass and lift it up. Your salami rose is ready to go.

CHOOSING & DISPLAYING CHEESES

Opinions differ on whether cheeses should be served whole or portioned on grazing boards. Pre-slicing your cheese fits the finger-food aesthetic of the classic grazing board, but whole cheeses can look spectacular. They add height, provide shape and colour, all of which can help create drama, flow, and energy on your board.

The type of cheese you're serving can be a deciding factor when it comes to how you serve it. Fresh cheeses, like goat's cheese, Burrata, or Panela are better served whole because they're messy to slice. Place them on your table in a dish, add a knife, and leave it up to your guests to attack.

Odd numbers of things look more attractive than even number groupings. One solitary cheese will look better than two, and three will look better than four.

If you're serving more than one cheese, make sure there are different types. A common combination is a soft or semi-soft cheese, a hard cheese, and a blue cheese, but don't feel like you have to stick rigidly to this mixture of textures and flavours. Just aim for some variety, whether that's a combination of fresh and aged cheeses or a mix of salty, nutty, and tangy cheeses.

One final thing to remember is that it will normally take cheese 20–30 minutes to come to room temperature. Give your cheese time to get to the perfect eating temperature before declaring the buffet open.

HOW TO SLICE CHEESES

How you slice your cheese depends on what it is. Different textures and shapes will look their best sliced in different ways.

Semi-soft & Semi-firm Cheeses

If the cheese is round, like a Brie, then halve it, turn it, and halve it again. Keep going in this way until you have 8–16 wedges, depending on how small you want to go. For other cheeses, follow the shape it arrived in. Wedges of queso añejo, Manchego, or Stilton can be sliced into triangles, while blocks of Havarti, Gouda, or Gruyère can be sliced into rectangles. Ball-shaped cheeses, like provolone and Edam, look good cut into thin rounds. Semi-firm cheeses are also great sliced into cubes and heaped in tumbling piles on your board.

Firm Cheeses

Aged firm cheeses are often dense with a crunchy crystallized texture that crumbles into thick flakes. If you're including cheeses like Parmesan, pecorino, or aged Cheddars, then use a sharp knife to slice shard-like chunks from the cheese. These flakes will look beautiful gathered together as part of your grazing board.

VEGETABLE CRUDITÉS

It's easy to get caught up in all the cured meats and rich cheeses that often form a major part of a grazing board, but including a range of fresh produce will bring balance and freshness to your platter. They're also essential for colour, and often help even out the costs.

Crudités are a the simplest way to make vegetables a part of your board. Crispy, crunchy vegetables like carrots, celery, cucumbers, radishes, and sugar snap peas are ideal served raw. Simply wash them, pat dry, and slice into batons (or leave smaller vegetables like radishes and sugar snaps whole). Baby carrots and cucumbers look very cute sliced in half (which will also save you a bit of chopping time).

Some veggies benefit from being lightly cooked. Asparagus, broccoli, cauliflower, and green beans can all be trimmed or broken into florets, then steamed or blanched to make them easier to eat. To blanch, cook them in boiling water for 1–2 minutes, then plunge them into a bowl of iced water to stop the cooking process. Transfer to a colander and leave to dry.

All the crudités can be included on your board without being paired with anything in particular, but it's nice to include at least one dip into which people can dunk them.

HOW TO MAKE CUCUMBER ROSES

You can make cucumber roses the same way you make salami roses, either by laying a row of overlapping cucumber circles on your work surface, then folding them in half and rolling up, or by using a glass to shape the rose around (see page 28). The important thing is to make sure your cucumber is as thinly sliced as possible – use a mandolin or the cutting tool on your food processor to get wafer-thin slices that can be easily folded.

FRUIT PLATTERS

Sweet and juicy fruits make a great addition to grazing platters. They're bright and cooling, and will refresh your palate in-between bites of salami.

Small fruits, such as blueberries, strawberries, blackberries, and cherries, are best left whole. Life is too short to carve petals into strawberries (unless you're being paid for it). Instead, use them as crevice-fillers, to fill in gaps amongst the larger items.

Medium-sized fruits, such as apples, pears, and peaches, are best cut into rounds or wedges. Remove any stones, stems, or pips, and dip the cut fruit into a little lemon juice. This will slow down the browning, but try to cut the fruit as close to serving time as possible. Oranges, kiwis, and figs, however, can be chopped into wedges or rounds and won't need dunking in lemon juice to keep them looking fresh.

Large fruits, such as melons, papayas, and pineapples, can be sliced into chunky wedges to create an eye-catching patch of colour on your board. Alternatively, use pastry cutters to cut smaller shapes out of the slices – you can use these to fill gaps on the board or pile them up in bowls.

Always leave bunches of grapes whole. They help recreate that Renaissance horn-of-plenty vibe, to which grazing boards are so well suited.

CREVICE-FILLERS & GARNISHES

Crevice-fillers are little foods that can fill in the gaps around the bigger, more structural items. Small fruits, like berries, are great crevice-fillers, as are cherry tomatoes and baby plum tomatoes. Nuts, such as pistachios, cashews, peanuts, pecans, walnuts, and hazelnuts, are brilliant for filling in gaps – just make sure you check for any allergies before adding them to your platter. Dried fruits, like apricots, figs, dates, and banana chips also work well.

Sweet treats and savoury snacks can be really useful for closing up spaces. Popcorn, sweets, toffees, fudge, nougat, and marshmallows can all be board-filling extras. Extra savoury snacks, such as mini breadsticks, mini cheese crackers, pretzels, cheese savouries, roasted chickpeas, puffed rice, and crispy fried lentils, don't just cover up voids, they add interesting texture and crunch.

A few sprigs or bundles of herbs will add a welcome splash of greenery to your board. Use woody herbs (like thyme, rosemary, and bay), as these will stay fresher for longer and won't wilt as the party progresses.

You can also use edible flowers as garnishes, but make sure they are definitely edible. Never put anything on your board that isn't safe to go in your mouth. Nasturtiums, pansies, cornflowers, rose petals, and herb flowers are all safe to eat and look gorgeous. Make sure you buy them from a grocer rather than a florist, as flowers grown for display can be sprayed with preservatives that are inedible. If you're not sure, leave them off your board.

HOW TO ADD SHINE BACK TO CHOCOLATE SNACKS

Chocolate-covered pretzels and biscuits are great crevice-fillers, but they can come out of the packet looking a little pale and dusty. To bring back the shine, warm your to 100°C/Fan 80°C/Gas Mark ¼. Line a baking tray with greaseproof baking paper and spread the pretzels or biscuits out onto the tray. Slide into the oven and warm for 1–3 minutes until the chocolate has just started to melt. Remove from the oven and set aside for a few hours. The chocolate will cool and harden, looking shiny and new.

PUTTING IT ALL TOGETHER

The first thing to remember is that the bigger the board, the more difficult it will be to carry. Building your board in situ means you can get the perfect look without worrying about ingredients rolling off when you try to transfer it from the kitchen to the table.

So first, get your board in the perfect spot. Once your board is in place, start by putting the largest items onto the board – typically, this will either be bowls or whole cheeses. Place your bowls or cheeses on the board, trying not to arrange them in a straight line. Instead, use these big ticket items to create points on a curve.

Next, add bulkier items to the board, such as large pieces of fruit, sliced cheeses, cured meats, crackers, and bread. Again, don't create defined groups or hard lines, but look for ways to hint at loops, twists, and spirals. Once all the large items are on the board, fill in the gaps with your crevice-fillers and garnishes.

Make sure you've added all the serving utensils you need, as well as any labels. Finally, arrange serving plates and napkins on the side. Your board is ready to be admired… and then demolished.

Butter Boards & Frosting Boards

How to Make a Butter Board

A simple savoury alternative to the grazing board is a butter board. They make a great appetizer. They are served with warm bread, which your guests use to scoop through the butter and its toppings.

Building a butter board is all about layers. Start with a base of softened unsalted butter. Beat it until light and creamy, then spread it over a dinner plate-sized board. The butter doesn't need to go right to the edges or look too neat and smooth. Use your butter knife to create rustic swirls and peaks, giving the butter dips and crevices in which flavours can gather.

The next layer should be a sprinkling of coarse sea salt, followed by any spices you'd like to add – toasted cumin or coriander seeds, fennel seeds, crushed chilli flakes, ground cinnamon, ground cardamom, freshly grated nutmeg, or fresh vanilla seeds are all good options. This is also a good point to add finely grated citrus zest.

Next, add your fresh ingredients. Finely chopped or shredded herbs, thinly sliced shallots or spring onions, diced vegetables, sliced chillies, roasted garlic cloves, chopped fruit, and edible flowers are all good options.

Finally, you can add a little crunch. For savoury butter boards, use a sprinkle of toasted breadcrumbs or crumbled crackers and breadsticks. For sweet boards, top with crushed meringues, chocolate chips, chopped nuts, or sprinkles.

How to Make a Frosting Board

The dessert equivalent of a butter board, a frosting board is normally made with buttercream frosting. This type of frosting holds it shape and won't melt or slide off the board. But you can make frosting boards with other sweet spreads, such as chocolate spread, nut butters, marshmallow fluff, or even a combination of jam and butter.

Like butter boards, the easiest way to build a frosting board is to start with a layer of frosting (or your other chosen spread) and then add layers of textures and flavours. Sprinkles, grated chocolate, chopped nuts, crystallized, or candied, fruit/fresh fruit, crumbled cookies or biscuits, and crushed sweets all make great additions to a frosting board.

An alternative way to present your frosting board is to dab the frosting onto the board using a palette knife. Scoop a little frosting on the end of the knife, then dab it down onto the board and gently drag to create a crescent of frosting. Repeat, lining the dabs up so they look like scales on a fish. You can do this with just one frosting, or mix it up with different flavours or combinations of spreads.

To serve, go for sugar cookies, crisp wafers, or individual sponges, like madeleines. Avoid chunks of sponge cake, as they will crumble when guests drag them through the frosting, leaving behind crumbs.

Quick & Delicious

The joy of grazing boards is that they're beautiful to look at and spectacular to eat, but you don't have to spend too much time stuck in the kitchen cooking. All the boards in this book come with a tailored recipe, so you can add a homemade dish to your platter if you want to make that extra effort. But there is a halfway house between cooking from scratch and using only ingredients you find at the deli counter, and this middle ground comes in the form of giving shop-bought ingredients a little upgrade.

Adding your own mix of herbs and spices to a jar of olives or packet of feta will elevate their flavours and ensure your boards are unique. To get you started, I've come up with some combinations for olives, feta, tofu, and butter. When you find a mix of flavours you like, start to experiment with similar ingredients until you have your own personal spice mix or marinade that makes your grazing board instantly recognizable.

MARINATED OLIVES

Olives are easy to marinate. They add colour and texture to your boards, and they love to soak up flavours – the perfect ingredient to start with when it comes to up-cycling shop-bought foods.

When picking your olives, go for brined olives that can be drained and rinsed before you add them to your marinade. Olives that haven't been stoned will last longer in the marinade and won't go mushy – just make sure there are dishes on the table into which guests can dispose of the stones.

Your first choice is whether to go for black or green olives (or a mix). The main difference between them – apart from the variety – is how ripe they are. Green olives left on the tree turn black as they ripen. This means that, usually, black olives are richer, smoother, and milder than green olives. They can be fruity or even a little sweet, and they normally go well with woody herbs, garlic, sun-dried tomatoes, and anchovies. Green olives tend to be crisp and tart, although they can also have a buttery-tasting flesh and floral notes. They usually go well with zingy spices, dried herbs, garlic, and citrus.

Some good varieties to start with include: fruity black Kalamata olives from Greece; buttery green Castelvetrano olives from Italy; smoky green Manzanilla olives from Spain; and nutty green Mission olives from the USA. Try soaking half your olives in one of these marinades and leaving the other half plain. Then put both on your board and see which one is the bigger hit.

Note: These olive dishes serve 4–8 people, depending on the rest of the board, and will keep well in the fridge for up to 1 week. Store them in sealed, airtight containers and marinate for 24 hours before serving. To serve, strain the olives and arrange in dishes, discarding any woody, chewy, and otherwise inedible aromatics.

LEMON, CHILLI & ROSEMARY

1 tsp dried chilli flakes
pared zest of 1 lemon
2 fat garlic cloves, sliced
3 short rosemary sprigs
250g olives in brine, drained and rinsed
50ml extra virgin olive oil

Place the chilli flakes, lemon zest, garlic, and rosemary in a mixing bowl. Add the olives with the olive oil. Stir to mix, then transfer to a tub, seal, and store in the fridge for 24 hours before serving. They will keep for up to 1 week.

SICHUAN CITRUS & GARLIC

2 tsp Sichuan peppercorns
pared zest of 1 lemon
pared zest of 1 orange
pared zest of 1 lime
2 long red chillies, halved
4 fat garlic cloves, sliced
250g olives in brine, drained and rinsed
50ml extra virgin olive oil

Toast the Sichuan peppercorns in a dry frying pan for 1–2 minutes until aromatic. Tip them into a mixing bowl and add the strips of lemon, orange, and lime zest. Add the chilli halves (leave the seeds and white pith in for spicy olives, or scoop them out if you want less heat), garlic, olives, and olive oil. Stir to mix, then transfer to a tub, seal, and store in the fridge for 24 hours before serving. They will keep for up to 1 week.

GRAPEFRUIT, BLACK PEPPER & ROSEMARY

2 tsp black peppercorns
pared zest of 1 grapefruit
3 short rosemary sprigs
250g olives in brine, drained and rinsed
50ml extra virgin olive oil

Toast the peppercorns in a dry frying pan for 1–2 minutes until aromatic. Tip into a mixing bowl and add the grapefruit zest and rosemary sprigs. Tip in the olives and pour in the olive oil. Stir to mix, then transfer to a tub, seal, and store in the fridge for 24 hours before serving. They will keep for up to 1 week.

ANCHOVY, THYME & GARLIC

3 anchovy fillets, finely chopped
6 short thyme sprigs
3 fat garlic cloves, sliced
250g olives in brine, drained and rinsed
50ml extra virgin olive oil

Place the chopped anchovy fillets in a mixing bowl. Add the thyme sprigs with the sliced garlic. Tip in the olives and pour in the olive oil. Stir to mix, then transfer to a tub, seal, and store in the fridge for 24 hours before serving. They will keep for up to 1 week.

MARINATED FETA

Cheese often has a starring role on grazing boards, and it doesn't normally need much fussing with to be fabulous. But if you're looking for a way to add extra spice, smoke, or zest, then feta is the cheese you need.

It's a semi-hard, crumbly cheese that is traditionally made with sheep's milk. It has a salty, sharp, and tangy flavour, and it's perfect if you want to add a savoury, creamy element to your grazing board. Marinate it, however, and within 30 minutes you have a rich, full-flavoured dish that will add variety and colour to your board.

When picking your feta, buy it in blocks packed in brine. You want a cheese that is firm enough to slice or break into chunks, but is not dry. Feta is a protected term and only cheeses made in Greece can be called feta.

Similar brined cheeses are made in other countries all around the world and these can work really well in the marinades (and are also often cheaper). The rule to apply when picking your cheese is: if you wouldn't eat it plain, then it isn't good enough to marinate.

Note: These marinated feta recipes serve 4–8 people, depending on the rest of the board, and will keep well in the fridge for up to 4 weeks. Store them in sealed, airtight containers and marinate for 24 hours before serving. To serve, strain the feta and arrange in dishes, discarding any woody, chewy, and otherwise inedible aromatics. The marinating oil makes a good dipping oil for bread, so pour it into bowls and serve alongside sliced, crusty bread as part of your board.

LEMON, BAY & THYME

2 shallots, very thinly sliced
400g feta, drained
350ml extra virgin olive oil, plus extra if needed
pared zest of 2 lemons
4 bay leaves
6 short thyme sprigs
2 tsp black peppercorns

If you have a mandolin, you can use that to slice the shallots to get really thin slices. Pat the drained feta dry with kitchen paper. Chop into 1–2-cm chunks.

Pour half the olive oil into a large container, then add half the shallots, lemon zest, bay, thyme, and peppercorns. Place the feta on top, then cover with the remaining aromatics and pour over the remaining oil. The oil should just cover the feta, so top up with a little extra if necessary.

Seal the container, then gently invert it a few times to mix the oil, feta, and aromatics. Marinate in the fridge for at least 24 hours before serving. It will keep in the fridge for up to 4 weeks.

SRIRACHA, PRESERVED LEMON & HONEY

350ml extra virgin olive oil, plus extra if needed
3 tbsp Sriracha
2 tbsp clear honey
½ preserved lemon (about 50g in weight)
4 fat garlic cloves, thinly sliced
2 spring onions, thinly sliced
400g feta, drained

Pour the olive oil into a mixing bowl and add the Sriracha and honey. Whisk together to combine. Scoop out the soft flesh from the preserved lemon half; discard the flesh, then dice the rind. Add the diced rind to the bowl with the garlic and spring onions, and whisk again.

Pat the drained feta dry with kitchen paper. Chop into 1–2-cm chunks.

Pour half the marinade into a large container and place the feta on top. Pour over the remaining marinade. The marinade should just cover the feta, so top up with a little extra olive oil, if necessary.

Seal the container, then gently invert it a few times to mix the oil, feta, and aromatics. Marinate in the fridge for at least 24 hours before serving. It will keep in the fridge for up to 4 weeks.

CHIPOTLE, LIME & CUMIN

2 tsp cumin seeds
2 tsp coriander seeds
1–2 tsp chipotle paste, to taste
350ml extra virgin olive oil, plus extra if needed
400g feta, drained
pared zest of 1 orange
pared zest of 2 limes
2 bay leaves

Toast the cumin and coriander seeds in a dry frying pan for 1–2 minutes until they are popping and aromatic. Tip into a mixing bowl. Add the chipotle paste and olive oil. Whisk to combine.

Pat the drained feta dry with kitchen paper. Chop into 1–2-cm chunks.

Pour half the chipotle oil into a container and add half the pared citrus zest and bay. Arrange the feta on top, then cover with the remaining aromatics and pour over the last of the chipotle oil. The marinade should just cover the feta, so top up with a little extra olive oil, if necessary.

Seal the container, then gently invert it a few times to mix the oil, feta, and aromatics. Marinate in the fridge for at least 24 hours before serving. It will keep in the fridge for up to 4 weeks.

MARINATED TOFU

If you're looking for a vegan alternative to feta, look no further than firmly pressed tofu. You can use the tofu in the same marinade mixes as the feta, or you can marinate it using the following recipe (see right) which results in the tofu having a similar taste and texture to feta. To make feta-style marinated tofu, you'll need to soak it for a minimum of 24 hours, but it's best after 48 hours.

This dish will serve 6–8 people, depending on the rest of the board, and it will keep for up to 2 weeks in the fridge in a sealed, airtight container.

FETA-STYLE MARINATED TOFU

450-g block extra-firm tofu, drained
100ml white wine vinegar
100ml freshly squeezed lemon juice
2 tbsp white miso paste
2 tbsp nutritional yeast
1 tbsp dried oregano
1 tbsp dried thyme
1 tsp garlic granules
½ tsp ground black pepper
fresh thyme and parsley (optional)

Put the drained tofu onto a plate lined with kitchen paper. Cover it with more kitchen paper, then place a small plate on top and weigh it down with a kitchen weight or a couple of tins. Leave the tofu for 30 minutes. Pressing it like this will help drain away any excess liquid. After 30 minutes, remove the weights and pat the tofu dry, then chop or tear it into 2-cm chunks.

In a bowl, whisk together the vinegar, lemon juice, miso paste, nutritional yeast, dried herbs, garlic granules, and black pepper. Pour half the marinade into a large container. Add the tofu, then pour over the remaining marinade. Seal and store in the fridge for 24–48 hours before serving. It will keep in the fridge for up to 2 weeks.

To serve, lift out of the marinade and arrange in a dish. You can scatter over fresh thyme leaves or chopped parsley to garnish.

FLAVOURED BUTTERS

One of the easiest ways to add variety to a simple charcuterie and cheese board is to include some good sliced bread and a flavoured butter. These butters are easy to make and they all have a really rich umami element that turns them into flavour bombs.

They will all keep in the fridge for 3–4 days, or you can freeze them for up to 1 month. To freeze in portions, let the butter set in the fridge, slice into rounds about 1 cm thick and open-freeze on a baking tray lined with greaseproof paper. Transfer to a container, layering them with more greaseproof paper, seal and store in the freezer. The butter will take 1–2 hours to defrost. Each recipe makes approximately 30 rounds, which is enough for 15–20 people.

SUN-DRIED TOMATO, BASIL & PARMESAN

250g lightly salted butter, softened
75g Parmesan, finely grated
50g sun-dried tomatoes in olive oil, drained and finely chopped
15g fresh basil leaves, shredded

Scoop the softened butter into a mixing bowl and beat with electric beaters until soft and creamy. Add the Parmesan, sun-dried tomatoes, and basil. Beat together until smoothly combined.

Scoop the butter onto a sheet of greaseproof paper and roll it round until you have a sausage shape. Wrap the paper around the butter, twisting the ends to seal. Chill for 1–2 hours to just set the butter. Now you can take the butter out of the fridge, unwrap it, and chop it into 10-cm lengths. Gently pat and roll into logs around 3 cm in diameter. Rewrap and chill overnight until firm. Either leave as logs, or slice each log into rounds about 1 cm thick.

ROAST GARLIC & PARSLEY

3 whole garlic bulbs
250g lightly salted butter, softened
15g fresh flat-leaf parsley, finely chopped
½ tsp ground black pepper
grated zest of 1 lemon
olive oil

Preheat the oven to 200°C/Fan 180°C/Gas Mark 6. Peel any loose papery skins off the garlic, then slice off the top quarter of the garlic bulbs, exposing the cloves, but keeping the bulb whole. Discard the tops of the bulbs and drizzle a little olive oil over each garlic bulb. Wrap them in foil and roast in the preheated oven for 25–30 minutes until soft and tender.

Let the garlic cool, then squeeze the soft garlic from the cloves into a mixing bowl, discarding the papery skins. Lightly crush the garlic with a fork, then add the softened butter and beat together until smooth. Add the chopped parsley to the bowl with the black pepper and lemon zest. Beat into the butter.

Scoop the butter onto a sheet of greaseproof paper and roll it round until you have a sausage shape. Wrap the paper around the butter, twisting the ends to seal. Chill for 1–2 hours to just set the butter. Now you can take the butter out of the fridge, unwrap it, and chop it into 10-cm lengths. Gently pat and roll into logs around 3 cm in diameter. Rewrap and chill overnight until firm. Either leave as logs, or slice each log into rounds about 1 cm thick.

WHITE MISO & SESAME
250g unsalted butter, softened
75g white miso paste
4–5 tbsp toasted sesame seeds

Scoop the softened butter into a mixing bowl and beat with electric beaters until soft and creamy. Add the white miso paste. Beat together until smoothly combined.

Scoop the butter onto a sheet of greaseproof paper and roll it round until you have a sausage shape. Wrap the paper around the butter, twisting the ends to seal. Chill for 1–2 hours to just set the butter. Now you can take the butter out of the fridge, unwrap it, and chop it into 10-cm lengths. Gently pat and roll into logs around 3 cm in diameter. Rewrap and chill overnight until firm.

Sprinkle the sesame seeds onto a plate and roll each log in them to coat lightly in seeds. Rewrap and chill overnight until firm. Either leave as logs, or slice into rounds about 1 cm thick.

SPICED MAPLE BUTTER
250g lightly salted butter, softened
150ml maple syrup
110g dark brown soft sugar
1 tsp ground cinnamon
1 tsp allspice
½ tsp ground cloves
½ tsp freshly grated nutmeg

Scoop the softened butter into a mixing bowl and beat with electric beaters until soft and creamy. Add the maple syrup and brown sugar. Beat together until smooth. Add the spices and beat again.

Scoop the butter onto a sheet of greaseproof paper and roll it round until you have a sausage shape. Wrap the paper around the butter, twisting the ends to seal. Chill for 1–2 hours to just set the butter. Now you can take the butter out of the fridge, unwrap it, and chop it into 10-cm lengths. Gently pat and roll into logs around 3 cm in diameter. Rewrap and chill overnight until firm. Either leave as logs, or slice each log into rounds about 1 cm thick.

Top 10 Tips

10 Tips to Build the Perfect Board

You've got your board, your bowls, and your cocktail sticks. You know how to slice cheese and you can make a salami rose. You're almost ready to start building your first grazing board. But before you start raiding your local delicatessen, read through these ten tips to building the perfect board. Following them will ensure that your grazing platter, no matter how big or small, turns out perfectly every time.

1 START WITH A LIST

When something involves a lot of elements, like a grazing board, lists keep you on track and make sure nothing is forgotten. Start with a list of your guests and any allergies they have. Work out what kinds of foods – and how much of them – you'll need, then make lists of all the ingredients and servingware you're going to use to build your board. Tick everything off as you go to make sure no cheese or salami rose gets left behind.

2 THINK IN THREE DIMENSIONS

Instagram normally shows grazing boards and tables from above, but your guests will definitely see them from the sides as well, so think about your grazing board in the round. Plan in ways to add height and create a flow of shapes. Bowls, raised boards, lazy Susans, and cake stands are all ways to make the landscape of your board varied and interesting.

3 MAKE GOOD USE OF COLOUR

Beautiful boards are bright and colourful. This can mean a rainbow mix of colours, combining two or three colours, or creating a board based around just one colour, like the Moody Blues Board (see page 165). Even if you're planning a board based around very beige food, such as chicken nuggets, you can add colour with bowls of sauce or slaw. And the colour doesn't just have to come from the food; colourful bowls, pretty cutlery, brightly hued napkins, and even the board itself can all generate a vibrant mix of tones.

4 THINK ABOUT THEMES

Grazing boards are known for being eclectic, but that doesn't mean they aren't themed. Think about the time of day you're serving your board, the kind of people who'll be eating, the time of year, and the sort of atmosphere you're trying to encourage, then plan your board to match that.

5 BALANCE THE FLAVOURS

The best boards contain a mix of four key flavours: salty, savoury, sweet, and spicy. Salty foods might include crisps, roasted nuts, pretzels, salty cheeses, and olives, while savoury foods include umami-rich treats like aged cheeses, meats, seafood, mushrooms, kimchi, and anchovies. For sweet flavours, think fruit, but also sweets, honey-roasted nuts, biscuits, wafers, and chocolate. Spicy includes chilli-flavoured foods and hot sauces, as well as dishes that make good use of your spice cupboard, such as marinated olives and cheeses, chutneys, and dipping sauces.

For a simple charcuterie board, balancing these flavours might include a dish of olives, an aged Cheddar, hams and salamis, grapes and figs, and a chutney. On a dessert board, the mix might include salted mini pretzels, breadsticks, strawberries, marshmallows, and a chocolate dipping sauce infused with cinnamon.

If you can't – or don't want to – include all four flavour elements, try to use a complementary combination of either sweet and salty or spicy and savoury. The contrast will make the food more interesting to eat and keep your guests coming back for more.

6 ADD IN TEXTURE

Alongside flavours, a variety of textures is a fantastic way to make sure your grazing board is appetizing. Combinations like breadsticks and dips, crackers and soft cheeses, or crudités and pâtés are satisfying to eat because we enjoy the mix of textures, so ensure you have a bit of both on your board.

7 PLAN YOUR PORTIONS

You never want your guests to go hungry, but equally you don't want to be left with half a deli counter after the party. Depending on what kind of board you're planning, the amount of different foods you'll need will vary, but these guidelines will help you calculate how much food to buy. These quantities are all per person (the lighter weights are for a grazing board as a starter, while the bigger weights are more main-meal sized), apart from the crackers and bread which should be counted per hour you expect each guest to be at your party.

Charcuterie: 50–150g
Cured Seafood: 50–100g
Cheeses: 85–180g
Fruit & Veg: 85–125g
Dips: 50–100g
Chocolate: 50–75g
Nuts, Crisps, Olives & Other Sundries: 75–115g
Bread & Crackers: 3–4 slices

8 KNOW YOUR TIMINGS

A charcuterie board for two will take around 10 minutes to create, while a grazing table for 40 might take two people 90 minutes to assemble. Be sensible about how much time it will take to create your board and build it into your party planning. This is especially important because grazing boards are at their best served as fresh as possible. You'll want to finish assembling your board just before your guests arrive, so plan ahead and don't get stuck dumping nuts and olives into bowls when you should be enjoying spending time with your guests.

Remember, you can prepare all the elements and have them ready to go, either in the fridge or in airtight containers on your

work surface. Go and get dressed for the party, then come back to your board, pop on an apron, and get creating. That way both you and your board will be party-ready when your guests arrive.

Also keep in mind how long you can leave your board out before you need to refresh it. Cheeses, cured meats, and seafood can typically be kept at room temperature for 4 hours before needing to be taken off the table. For large parties that you expect to go on for a few hours, it's sensible to keep around one-third of the temperature-sensitive foods in the fridge, so you can refresh the table halfway through the party.

9 BE PRACTICAL

A bacon and pancakes breakfast board for 50 sounds amazing, but unless you have an army of helpers and hot plates it will be a nightmare to serve. Even if you do manage to get all the food out onto the board hot, there will be guests who end up with a plate of cold, flabby pancakes. Be practical when deciding what kind of board to serve and take into account how many guests there are, how much time you actually have to create the board, and what your budget realistically is.

10 REMEMBER THIS IS MEANT TO BE FUN

If it's 2 a.m. the night before the party and you're still threading mini mozzarella balls and cherry tomatoes onto skewers, then something has gone very wrong. Grazing boards are meant to be a fun way to share food with your friends and family. Don't over-commit, spread the work around, and make sure you can grab a plate, fill it up, and tuck into the food along with everyone else. After all, a happy host makes for happy guests and a good party.

Glorious
Boards

Breakfast & Brunch

American Breakfast Board

This breakfast board has plenty of flair, largely due to the pops of colour provided by the mix of fruit. You can use any mix of fruit you like, just allow around 150g per person. The secret to making this breakfast board work is having all the fruit prepared and the pancakes and bacon cooked and being kept warm in the oven. Then, when your guests have emerged from their bedrooms and are pouring themselves their first cup of coffee, you can put it all together in under 5 minutes, ready for them to help themselves. It's perfect for special occasions, like Christmas or Mother's Day, or for turning an ordinary Sunday into something special.

Serves 6

24 Buttermilk Pancakes (see right)
18 rashers streaky bacon
125ml maple syrup
90g blueberries
125g raspberries
125g blackberries
180g strawberries
180g pineapple chunks
1 apple, cored and sliced
1 peach, stoned and sliced
90g butter, cubed
fresh mint sprigs, to garnish

Make the buttermilk pancakes following the recipe right and keep them warm in the oven. Grill the bacon and keep it warm alongside the pancakes.

Place a bowl on the board and pour in the maple syrup. Arrange the pancakes and bacon on the board, and then fill in the gaps with the fruit. Add the butter to the board, garnish with mint sprigs, and serve straight away.

BUTTERMILK PANCAKES

Makes 24

25g unsalted butter, plus extra for greasing
150g plain flour
1 tsp baking powder
50g caster sugar
a pinch of sea salt
2 medium eggs
110ml buttermilk (see Buttermilk Alternative below)

Melt the butter and set it aside to cool. Sift the flour and baking powder into a large mixing bowl. Add the sugar with a pinch of salt. Whisk to mix all the dry ingredients together.

Beat the eggs and buttermilk together in a separate bowl, then add them to the dry ingredients and whisk to combine. Pour in the melted butter and whisk again. You should have a thick batter the consistency of double cream. Cover the bowl with a clean tea towel and set aside to rest for 20 minutes.

Set your oven to its lowest setting and put an ovenproof plate in there to keep warm. Give the batter a quick whisk to make sure it's smooth.

Warm a frying pan over a medium–high heat. Grease it with a little butter, then add 2 tablespoons batter per pancake to the pan. Fry for 2–3 minutes until bubbles start to form on the top and they look set, then flip them over and cook for a further 1–2 minutes until set and browned. Transfer to the plate in the oven to keep warm. Repeat until you have used all your batter. Serve warm.

Buttermilk alternative: If you don't have buttermilk, stir 1 tablespoon lemon juice into 110ml milk and let it sit for 5–10 minutes until it looks curdled. This acidifies the milk, which will help make your pancakes fluffy. If you need more buttermilk, increase the quantities as needed.

Sugar Waffles Brunch Board

Crisp, fluffy sugar waffles are Belgium's finest export and they're easy to make at home. I've paired them with a mixture of berries and a sweet fruit compote, but you could serve them with bacon and maple syrup; strawberries and Nutella; or caramelized bananas, ice cream, and chocolate sauce (which would make this more of a dessert board). The berries on this board include myrtle berries, which are available in the autumn and have a tart, tangy flavour – you may want to serve some honey alongside them. If you can't get myrtle berries, double up the blueberries and garnish with mint leaves.

Serves 6

12 Vanilla Sugar Waffles (see right)
350g berry compote
200g strawberries
125g blueberries
125g myrtle berries
myrtle leaves and edible flowers, to garnish

Make the vanilla sugar waffles following the recipe right and keep them warm in the oven.

Place a bowl for the berry compote on the board and spoon it in. Arrange the fruit and waffles around the compote. Garnish with a few myrtle leaves and edible flowers. Serve straight away.

VANILLA SUGAR WAFFLES

Makes 12

100g unsalted butter
500g plain flour
4 tsp baking powder
100g caster sugar
a pinch of sea salt
550ml buttermilk (see Buttermilk Alternative, page 74)
4 medium eggs, separated
4 tsp vanilla extract

waffle iron

Melt the butter and set aside to cool. Sift the flour and baking powder into a large mixing bowl. Add the sugar and a pinch of salt. Whisk to mix the dry ingredients together.

Pour the buttermilk into a separate bowl. Add the egg yolks (keeping the whites for later) and vanilla. Whisk to combine.

Add a splash of the buttermilk mixture to the dry ingredients and whisk in to make a thick paste. Slowly whisk in the remaining buttermilk until you have a smooth, thick batter. Whisk in the melted butter. Cover the bowl with a clean tea towel and set aside for 30 minutes to rest.

When the batter has rested for 20 minutes, place the egg whites in a clean, grease-free, non-plastic bowl and whisk until it forms soft peaks. Fold the egg whites into the fully rested batter with a metal spoon, trying not to knock out too much air.

Set your oven to its lowest temperature and pop an ovenproof plate in there to keep warm. Grease your waffle irons and cook the batter following the manufacturer's instructions, transferring them to the oven to keep warm. Serve straight away.

Continental Breakfast Board

One of the best things about staying at a hotel is the breakfast buffet. Trekking between food stations, choosing which cheeses, cured meats, pickles, eggs, pastries, and bread to pile up on your plate is always a pleasure. You can recreate the magic of a lazy morning grazing at a European guesthouse with this Continental breakfast board. It is full of fresh flavours, thanks to the chilli-spiced gremolata and the crisp fruit and veg, as well as some popular meats and cheeses. As ever, you can mix things up by swapping in different cheeses or using cold charcuterie instead of grilled sausages.

Serves 4

50g Spicy Gremolata (see right)
4 boiled eggs, peeled and halved (see The Perfect Boiled Egg see box, right)
150g Houmous (see page 120 or use ready-made)
4 kielbasa
150g cherry tomatoes on the vine
8 small crusty bread rolls
200g olives, drained
80g sun-dried tomato chutney
80g cherry jam
½ cucumber, sliced
150g Gouda, sliced
230g Petit Reblochon
100g radishes
150g strawberries
a bunch of flat-leaf parsley

Prepare the spicy gremolata and boiled eggs following the instructions right, and prepare the houmous (if making your own). Grill the kielbasa and cherry tomatoes on the vine. Warm the bread rolls.

Place the bowl of gremolata on the board. Add a few more bowls or jars and spoon in the houmous, olives, chutney, and cherry jam. Add the sliced cucumber, cheeses, warm bread rolls, boiled eggs, grilled kielbasa, and grilled tomatoes. Fill in the gaps with the radishes, strawberries, and flat-leaf parsley.

SPICY GREMOLATA

a bunch of flat-leaf parsley, finely chopped
2 garlic cloves, very finely chopped
1 long red chilli, finely chopped
grated zest of 1 lemon, plus a squeeze of juice
sea salt and freshly ground black pepper

Combine all the ingredients in a bowl, mix well, and adjust the seasoning to taste.

THE PERFECT BOILED EGG

Whether you prefer hard- or soft-boiled eggs, the secret to cooking them is getting the water to the right temperature, setting your timer, and then chilling the eggs (if you want to peel them). Three simple steps to the perfect breakfast egg.

Get a pan of water boiling, then add your eggs to the boiling water straight from the fridge.

Turn the heat down so the pan is gently simmering and cook the eggs for 10 minutes for hard-boiled, or for 7 minutes if you want eggs with jammy, semi-set yolks. Lift them out of the water with a slotted spoon. You can serve them warm with toast at this stage.

To peel them, move the eggs straight from the pan to a bowl of iced water. Leave them for 15–30 minutes to cool completely. If you have time, leave them overnight. Drain the eggs and gently pull away the shells, trying not to peel off any white with the eggshell. Rinse under cold water, halve, and drain briefly on kitchen paper. They're ready to serve.

Healthy Start Morning Board

If you've ever thought your family aren't eating enough fruit, then this breakfast board will convince them to tuck in. There's a piece of fruit on the board that is sure to appeal to everyone, from sharp and zesty grapefruit to juicy mango and sweet banana. As with all the breakfast boards, you can vary the fruit to suit your tastes and the time of year. Just add a good, thick yoghurt and some granola for crunch.

Serves 4

150g Honey & Nut Granola (see right)
600g Greek yoghurt
1 mango, stoned and sliced
1 grapefruit, sliced into wedges
1 banana, peeled and sliced
2 kiwi fruit, halved or sliced
2 figs, quartered
1 peach, stoned and sliced
50g blueberries
80g raspberries
a small bunch of grapes

Make the granola following the recipe right.

Place a bowl for the yoghurt on your board and spoon in the yoghurt. Arrange the fruit on the board around it.

Just before you serve, heap the granola up on the board, using it to fill the gaps – it will start to go soggy when it's in contact with cut fruit, so add it last. Serve straight away.

HONEY & NUT GRANOLA

Makes 1kg

250g porridge oats
250g barley flakes
200g mixed nuts, roughly chopped
50g pumpkin or sunflower seeds
1 tbsp ground cinnamon
1 tbsp mixed spice
150g coconut oil or unsalted butter
175ml clear honey

Preheat the oven to 180°C/Fan 160°C/Gas 4. Place the oats and barley flakes in a large bowl. Stir in the chopped nuts, seeds, ground cinnamon, and mixed spice.

Warm the oil/butter and honey in a pan until melted and combined. Pour into the oats and stir to mix thoroughly.

Spread the granola over 1–2 large baking trays, making sure it forms a flat, even layer. Bake for 20–30 minutes, stirring every 10 minutes to turn the granola over, until golden brown.

Let the granola cool, then transfer to a sterilized jar (see box, below) and seal. The granola will keep for around 4 weeks.

Mix it up: You can use your favourite nut for this granola, or use a mix. Hazelnuts, walnuts, pecans, and almonds are all good picks.

HOW TO STERILIZE A JAR

To sterilize a glass jar, preheat the oven to 160°C/Fan 140°C/Gas 3. Wash the jar in hot, soapy water (including the lid, if it has one), then rinse and place on a baking tray. Slide into the oven and heat for around 15 minutes. Remove from the oven and leave to cool until cold enough to handle.

Smoked Salmon & Bagels Breakfast Platter

This breakfast board is a master class in no-cook elegance. It will take 20 minutes to put together – less if you're not soaking the onions – and although the ingredients are relatively simple, they convey a sense of luxury and indulgence when they're put together. The flair you create when arranging them on the board only adds to that. This is a great board for brunching with friends, especially accompanied by mimosas, or for serving at business breakfasts.

Serves 4

1 red onion, thinly sliced
200g cream cheese
20g capers, rinsed
400g smoked salmon
1 lemon, sliced
1 beef tomato, sliced
½ cucumber, thinly sliced
50g radishes, trimmed and thinly sliced
4 bagels
fresh basil and thyme sprigs, to garnish

Add the onion slices to a bowl of iced water and soak for 15 minutes. This will help mellow the onion's pungency. After 15 minutes, drain and lightly pat dry with kitchen paper. If you want to keep the onion punchy, skip this step.

Place the bowls for the cream cheese and capers on the board and fill them up. Arrange the smoked salmon on the board, then arrange the sliced lemon, tomato, red onion, cucumber, and radishes on the board around them.

Toast the bagels. Tuck a few fresh herb sprigs on the board to garnish and serve straight away with the warm bagels.

FLAVOUR SWAPS

Smoked salmon, bagels, and cream cheese form a classic combo, but they're not the only bagels in town. If you have vegetarian guests, fish-haters, or just want to make this board work better for your budget, swap the smoked salmon for one of these bagel fillings. They will all go beautifully with the cream cheese and veg.

Smoked trout: This freshwater fish has a delicate, gamey flavour and is usually less salty-tasting than smoked salmon. It has a similar, pretty pink colour and is a good option if you're looking for a more affordable smoked fish for your breakfast board.

Grilled portobello mushrooms: Always a go-to when you want a veggie alternative to animal protein. Rub whole portobello mushrooms with a splash of soy sauce, some garlic granules, and a pinch of smoked paprika, then grill until juicy.

Grilled red peppers: Make life easy by using jars of roasted peppers. Alternatively, grill a mix of red, yellow, and green peppers until the skin has charred, let them cool, then peel off the blistered skin, slice, and serve.

Avocado: Seems counterintuitive, but pairing rich avocado with cream cheese does work, especially if you keep the fresh, crunchy veg on the board. To make it look beautiful, shape the avocado into a rose (see page 93).

Pastrami: Give your board a New York deli makeover and swap in slices of pastrami. Keep the cream cheese, but have a dish of mustard instead of capers and change the lemon slices to pickled gherkins.

Snacks &
Starters

Easy Antipasti Board

The OG, or original, grazing board of the grazing board world, the antipasti board is a celebration of Italian cured meats and cheeses. It's inspired by the small snacks that are served alongside aperitivo drinks in Italy. In those golden hours between work and dinner, you can unwind with a Spritz and some choice bites that will warm your stomach up for the meal that's to come. This mini board is the perfect size for four people to share over a drink before dinner, or it would make a simple, light meal for two.

Serves 2–4

8 Grissini (see right)
8 slices prosciutto di Parma
100g Parmesan
100g olives, drained
6 slices salami Milano
12 slices fennel salami (Salamino Finocchiona)
6 slices coppa or bresaola
fresh basil sprigs, to garnish

Make the grissini following the recipe right. When the breadsticks have cooled, take 1 slice of prosciutto di Parma and wrap it around 1 breadstick. Repeat until you've used up the prosciutto. Use a cheese knife to break the Parmesan into bite-sized chunks.

Place the bowl for the olives onto the board and spoon them in. Arrange the prosciutto-wrapped grissini, the Parmesan, the salamis, and the coppa/bresaola on the board. Garnish with fresh basil and serve.

GRISSINI

Makes 25

350g strong white flour
½ tsp fine salt
½ tsp caster sugar
7g fast-action dried yeast
100ml olive oil
150ml warm (hand-hot) water
flaky sea salt, to sprinkle

2 large baking trays, lined with baking paper

Sift the flour into a large mixing bowl. Add the salt, sugar, and yeast. Whisk to mix all the dry ingredients together.

Pour in the olive oil and warm water. Use your hand to mix it all together until it forms a ball. Turn out onto your work surface and knead for around 10 minutes until the dough is supple and elastic. Alternatively, use a stand mixer and a dough hook to make the dough. Transfer the dough to a clean bowl, cover with a tea towel, and leave to rise for 1 hour.

Preheat the oven to 240°C/Fan 220°C/Gas 9.

Knock the dough back to deflate it, then pull off a small chunk, weighing around 20g. Pop it onto a clean work surface and roll it with the palms of your hands to make a long, thin breadstick around 25 cm long – don't flour the work surface, you need the friction to help shape the grissini into long sticks. Place the breadstick on the lined baking tray, then repeat with the rest of the dough. You should make around 25 grissini. Sprinkle a few pinches of flaky sea salt over them.

Slide the trays into the oven and bake for 12–15 minutes until the grissini are golden brown and feel light if you pick one up (protect your hands with an oven glove). Transfer to a wire rack and let them cool. They will keep in an airtight tin for 2–3 days.

Brimming Bruschette Board

Closer to a classic canapé tray than a grazing board, this collection of bruschette makes a great starter for informal dinners, or snacks to enjoy alongside evening drinks. If you want to turn it into more of a grazing board, make your bruschette toasts and then arrange your choice of toppings in bowls, shape them into elegant fans and ribbons, and pile them in artful heaps on a platter. Your guests can then pick and choose the toppings for their bruschette, mixing and matching their favourites. These bruschette are best made in the summer, when tomatoes are at their sweetest and juiciest.

Serves 3–6

6 slices Bruschette Toasts (see right)
2 tbsp basil pesto
½ tbsp extra virgin olive oil
25g Parmesan
300g really good tomatoes, such as San Marzano, roughly chopped
flaky sea salt, to sprinkle
6 slices prosciutto di Parma
1–2 tbsp good-quality balsamic vinegar
2–3 fresh basil sprigs

Make the bruschette toasts following the recipe right.

Spoon the pesto into a bowl and add the olive oil. Stir to mix – you want to thin it out a little so it's easy to drizzle. Use a small sharp knife to slice the Parmesan into flakes.

Place the bruschette toasts on your board. Top half of them with the roughly chopped tomatoes. Drizzle over the pesto and sprinkle over a little flaky sea salt. Top the other half of the bruschette toasts with the Parmesan. Softly drape the prosciutto over the cheese, then drizzle over a little balsamic vinegar.

Pick the basil leaves off the sprigs and dot them over the bruschette to garnish. Serve within 30 minutes of being made.

BRUSCHETTE TOASTS
Makes 6

6 slices sourdough bread, around 1 cm thick
3–4 tbsp olive oil

Preheat the oven to 180°C/Fan 160°C/Gas Mark 4. Place the sourdough slices on a baking tray and drizzle over the olive oil. Turn the bread over several times, making sure you rub as much olive oil into the bread as possible.

Bake in the oven for 15–20 minutes, turning the bread over after 10 minutes. The toasts are ready when they're golden brown and crisp. Set aside to cool for a few minutes before using to make bruschette.

Add char: Baking the toasts in the oven ensures they are evenly crisp and are a fairly uniform, golden-brown colour. If you'd prefer char marks, place the bread on your work surface and drizzle over the oil. Turn the bread to coat it. Heat a griddle pan and add the oiled bread. Cook for 2–3 minutes on each side until crisp and lightly charred.

Secretly Simple Charcuterie Board

This pan-European grazing board is a perfectly balanced mix of sweet and salt. The three cheeses and the richly savoury charcuterie are matched by the honey and the syrupy sweetness of dried figs, along with the refreshing juiciness of the grapes. It's an easy board to put together and not too heavy, which makes it a great board to share with friends before a meal. The tarallini are a fun element on the board, adding texture and shape. These small, round, crunchy snacks come from Puglia in southern Italy. You can swap them for mini breadsticks or pretzels, or even a few handfuls of crisps, if you can't get hold of them in your local shop.

Serves 6

12 slices salami Milano
6 slices cooked ham
90ml clear honey
100g Cheddar, cubed
100g Gorgonzola Dolce, cubed
200g petit Brie de Meaux, sliced
a small bunch of grapes
3–4 dried figs, sliced
100g tarallini
36 savoury crackers

Make a salami rose (see page 28) with the salami Milano. Roll the slices of cooked ham into loose rolls.

Place the salami rose on your board, along with a bowl for the honey. Pour in the honey.

Arrange the rolls of cooked ham, sliced and cubed cheeses, and the bunch of grapes on the board, then fill in the gaps with the sliced dried figs, tarallini, and crackers. Serve within 1 hour of being made.

MATCHING CHEESES WITH HONEY

Honey is not the most obvious condiment jar to pull out of your pantry when you're putting together a cheeseboard, but combining sweet with salty is always a winning move. A mild, all-purpose honey is always a safe bet, but if you want to add interesting layers of flavour, try matching different types of cheese to different kinds of honey.

- **Chestnut honey:** Good with nutty, full-flavoured cheeses like Parmesan, Manchego, and Comté

- **Heather honey:** Serve with crumbly, mature cheeses such as Cheddar, Lancashire, and Old Amsterdam

- **Blossom honey:** Pair with creamy, semi-soft cheeses like Taleggio, Reblochon, and Brie

- **Wildflower honey:** Match with piquant blue cheeses, such as Roquefort, Stilton, and Cabrales

- **Lavender honey:** Try with soft goat's and sheep's cheeses

- **Honeycomb:** A great all-rounder that goes well with most cheeses and will look spectacular on your grazing board

Gorgeous Green Grazing Plate

Not every grazing board has to be centred around cheese and charcuterie. This gloriously green collection of fruit and veg looks like it was picked fresh from the garden. It's a refreshing mix of ingredients that still holds true to the principle of balancing sweet, savoury, spicy, and salty. There's sweetness from the kiwi and pears, and savouriness provided by the rich avocado, while the rocket and mustard cress gives the board a peppery kick. A simple French vinaigrette brings it all together. This is a vibrant way to start a meal. It's also a stunning way to serve a side salad.

Serves 4

1 Avocado Rose (see right)
2 pears, cored
1 cucumber
25g rocket
2 kiwi fruit, peeled and sliced
1 lime, cut into wedges
a handful of mustard cress
1 tbsp extra virgin olive oil
1 tbsp white wine vinegar
1 tsp Dijon mustard
1 tsp clear honey (replace honey with maple syrup to make this board vegan)
sea salt and freshly ground black pepper
1–2 tsp poppy seeds

Make an avocado rose following the instructions right. Cut one of the pears into wedges and one into thin slices. Use a vegetable peeler to peel the cucumber into thin ribbons.

Arrange the rocket on your board, plate, or bowl, and add the avocado rose. Arrange all the fruit and veg around the rose, adding a handful of mustard cress. In a mixing bowl, whisk together the oil, vinegar, mustard, and honey with a pinch of salt and pepper. Taste the dressing and add a pinch more salt and pepper, if you think it needs it. Drizzle the dressing over the salad and scatter over the poppy seeds. Serve within 30 minutes.

HOW TO MAKE AN AVOCADO ROSE

Makes 1

You will need 1 ripe avocado. It should be firm, but with a little give. Too soft and it will turn to mush as you slice and shape it.

Start by halving your avocado. Set the half with the stone in to one side. If the avocado has a stem button at the top, remove that. Then place it cut-side down on your board and carefully pull away the skin. Brush a little lemon juice over the avocado and gently use your fingers to smooth out any dimples.

Slice the avocado very thinly, cutting across the avocado. Try to make the slices as similar sized as possible. Gently fan the slices out, sliding them to create a single line, with each slice just overlapping the slice next to it, then slowly shape that line into a horseshoe.

Now take the narrowest end of the line and gently roll it inwards to create a spiral. As you curl the slices towards to centre, it will start to look like a rose. Slide a spatula underneath the rose and transfer it to your grazing board.

You can make a second rose using the other avocado half, but because you've had to scoop out the stone the centre will be a little mushy and it won't hold as well.

Kids' Snack Tray

Whether it's a play date or a party, ensuring children are well fuelled can be the difference between a group of kids happily having fun together and a squabbling gang of marauders. If the children are old enough to eat without supervision, then a grazing board is a great way to feed kids without interrupting their play and allow them the agency to choose what they want to eat (from your carefully curated selection, of course). Depending on the ages of the children, this board will feed between four and eight hungry mouths. You can customize the sandwich fillings to suit your little ones, and experiment with different snacks. A mix of fresh fruit or veggies on the board adds colour and texture, as well as good nutrition. For children's parties, a row of these boards on the buffet table will look fabulous.

Serves 4–8

24 Sandwich Roll-ups (see right)
4–8 Sandwich Pockets (see right)
4 apples, cored and sliced
2 bananas, peeled and sliced
50g plain popcorn
50g square or mini pretzels

Make the sandwich roll-ups and pockets following the instructions right.

Arrange the sandwiches on the board, then add the sliced apples and bananas. Fill in the gaps with the popcorn and pretzels. Serve within 1 hour of assembling.

SANDWICH ROLL-UPS

Also known as pinwheels, these mini sandwich bites are great for kids, but grown-ups will also enjoy eating them.

To make them, take a slice of bread and cut off the crusts. Spread the bread with butter, cream cheese, or mayonnaise (or jam if you want to make sweet sandwiches), then top with a fine layer of something like grated cheese, very thinly sliced ham or pastrami, shredded roast chicken, little gem lettuce leaves, or fresh herbs (or grated chocolate or sprinkles for sweet). If there is any excess filling hanging over the edge of the bread, trim it off.

Roll the bread up like a sausage, then wrap tightly in cling film or beeswax paper and twist the ends to seal. Chill for 2 hours or overnight. To serve, remove the wrapper and slice into rounds. You should get 4–6 roll-ups, depending on how thickly you slice them. Serve within 1 hour of being sliced.

SANDWICH POCKETS

Not everybody loves crusts. Those people – big or small – who prefer their sandwich made with just the fluffy bit of the bread will enjoy these crustless pockets. And, because they're sealed, there's less chance of the filling falling out when they bite in.

To make them, slice the crusts off 2 slices of bread and spread them with butter, cream cheese, or mayonnaise (or jam if you want to make sweet pockets). Top one slice with another filling or two, like grated cheese, shredded roast chicken, diced grilled veggies, or flaked tuna (or sliced banana, strawberries, or grated chocolate for sweet pockets). Cover with the other slice, then use a fork to crimp the edges together. Serve within 1 hour of making.

Fabulous Four Butter Boards

The new kid on the grazing-board block, butter boards are an easy way to finesse your dinner party without going to the trouble of making origami ham. Their beauty lies in their simplicity – a thick layer of creamy butter enhanced by a mix of full-flavoured toppings that you eat by sweeping a slice of crusty bread through it. If you want to build your own butter board, turn to page 42 where there's a guide to putting one together. If you prefer to start out with some inspiration, try making one of these butter boards. There are three savoury suggestions and one sweet to try before branching out on your own.

All recipes below serve 8

BROCCOLI, ANCHOVY & HAZELNUT BUTTER BOARD

50g broccoli florets
250g Green Butter (see right), softened
8 anchovy fillets, drained
25g hazelnuts, roughly chopped
a pinch of sea salt

Lightly steam or simmer the broccoli florets for 2–3 minutes until just tender. Drain and set aside to cool.

Make the green butter following the recipe and place it in a mixing bowl. Lightly beat until creamy and spreadable. Use a spatula to swirl the butter onto a plate.

Chop the broccoli into small florets and dot them over the green butter. Arrange the anchovy fillets on the butter, then sprinkle over the hazelnuts and a pinch of salt. Serve within 30 minutes of assembling.

GREEN BUTTER

Makes 250g

30g fresh flat-leaf parsley
1 tbsp fresh thyme leaves
2 tbsp fresh sage leaves
25g baby spinach leaves
200g unsalted butter, softened
a pinch of sea salt (optional)

Place the parsley (leaves and stalks) in a food processor. Add the thyme leaves, sage leaves, and baby leaf spinach. Blitz until finely chopped.

Dice the butter and add to the processor. Blitz until blended. You can add a generous pinch of sea salt now, or save it to sprinkle on top of the butter before serving (optional).

Scoop the butter onto a sheet of greaseproof paper and roll it round until you have a sausage shape. Wrap the paper around the butter, twisting the ends to seal. Chill for 1–2 hours to just set the butter. Now you can take the butter out of the fridge, unwrap it, and chop into 10-cm lengths. Gently pat and roll into logs around 3 cm in diameter. You can keep the butter in the fridge for 3–4 days or freeze for up to 1 month.

Place the butter in a mixing bowl and lightly beat until creamy and spreadable. Use a spatula to swirl the butter onto a plate.

Scatter the roughly chopped figs and pecans over the butter. Drizzle over some honey and sprinkle over a little flaky sea salt. Serve within 30 minutes of assembling.

LEMON, CHIVE & PARMESAN BUTTER BOARD

250g unsalted butter, softened
finely grated zest of 1 lemon
20g Parmesan
a small handful of chives, finely chopped
flaky sea salt, to sprinkle

Place the butter in a mixing bowl and lightly beat until creamy and spreadable. Use a spatula to swirl the butter onto a plate.

Sprinkle the lemon zest over the butter. Use a vegetable peeler to thinly slice the Parmesan into flakes and scatter the Parmesan flakes over the butter. Sprinkle over the finely chopped chives and a small pinch of flaky sea salt. Serve within 30 minutes of assembling.

FRESH FIG, HONEY & PECAN BUTTER BOARD

250g unsalted butter, softened
2 figs, roughly chopped
25g pecans, roughly chopped
1–2 tbsp clear honey
flaky sea salt, to sprinkle

ANTIPASTI BUTTER BOARD

250g salted butter, softened
4–6 slices salami Napoli
¼ red onion, thinly sliced
8–10 pitted green olives, drained and
    roughly chopped
a small handful of rocket

Place the butter in a mixing bowl and lightly beat until creamy and spreadable. Use a spatula to swirl the butter onto a plate.

Slice the salami into three pieces each. Top the butter with the salami, red onion, and olives. Scatter over a few rocket leaves. Serve within 30 minutes of assembling.

Everyday Celebrations

Harvest Home Cheese & Charcuterie Board

If you want a fuss-free board that's guaranteed to be a crowd-pleaser, look no further than this pan-European platter. The cheeses are the big draw: four mild and creamy French cheeses that are gorgeous served with fresh, crusty bread, fig chutney, and homemade pickled pears. To go with the cheeses, there are two meats: the ever-popular chorizo and jambon de Bayonne. This air-dried ham comes from the south-west of France and it has a delicate, slightly nutty flavour and a melt-in-the-mouth texture. The remaining ingredients, including the sauerkraut, caper berries, and grilled peppers, should be available in large supermarkets or delis.

Serves 6

250g Pickled Pears (see right)
100g half petit Brie de Meaux
150g each Saint Agur blue cheese, Port Salut
   and Sainte-Maure de Touraine goat's cheese
400g sliced jambon de Bayonne
300g sliced chorizo
460-g jar roasted peppers in olive oil, drained
125g sauerkraut, drained
250g fig chutney
90g wholegrain mustard
90g caper berries, drained
250g green olives, drained
190-g jar cornichons, drained
a few small bunches of grapes
1 medium sourdough loaf, sliced
1 baguette, sliced
54 wheat crackers
nasturtium leaves, to garnish

Make the pickled pears, following the recipe. Arrange the cheeses and meats on the board. Place bowls on the board and fill them with the pears, peppers, sauerkraut, chutney, mustard, caper berries, and olives. Fill in the gaps with the smaller items. Garnish with nasturtium leaves. Serve within 1 hour of assembling.

PICKLED PEARS
Makes 1kg

pared zest of 1 orange
4 star anise
2 tsp black peppercorns
1 tbsp green cardamom pods
1 cinnamon stick, snapped in half
6-cm piece of fresh ginger, peeled and thinly sliced
800ml white wine vinegar
800g caster sugar
2kg pears, peeled, quartered, and cored

Place all the ingredients apart from the pears in a medium-sized pan and set it over a medium–low heat. Gently warm until the sugar has dissolved.

When the sugar has dissolved, add the pear quarters to the pan and turn the heat up a little. Gently simmer for 10–15 minutes until the pears are just tender – you should be able to push a skewer through a pear easily without it falling apart.

Lift the pears out of the pan with a slotted spoon and transfer them to a sterilized, 1-litre jar (see page 81 for instructions on how to sterilize a jar).

Turn the heat up and boil the pickling liquid for 5–10 minutes until it has reduced by a third and become syrupy. Ladle the liquid over the pears, seal the jar, and set aside somewhere cool and dark for 1 month before using. The pickled pears will keep well for 6–8 months. Once opened, store in the fridge and use within 1 month.

All Around the Med Feast

Take a tour of the Mediterranean with this plant-led grazing board. This culinary tour encompasses flavours from across the Med, including Turkish dolmas (stuffed vine leaves) and Italian grissini through to sweet Spanish almonds and tangy Greek olives. This board is perfect for al fresco eating, or any relaxed light meal that you want to share with family and friends. All the elements are served at room temperature, so everything can be prepared in advance. You just bring the board to the table, then relax in the warm glow of the Mediterranean sunshine (real or imagined) and enjoy.

Serves 4

8 Dolmas (see overleaf)
8 Grissini (see page 86 or use ready-made)
8 Bruschette Toasts (see page 89 or use ready-made)
1 aubergine, sliced into rounds
olive oil, for brushing
100g Kalamata olives
460-g jar roasted peppers in olive oil, drained
100g pistachios
50g almonds
125g baby plum tomatoes
60g caper berries, drained
80g sun-dried tomatoes
fresh sage and thyme sprigs, to garnish

Make the dolmas, following the recipe overleaf. If you're making the grissini and bruschette toasts, follow the recipes on page 86 and 89.

Heat the grill to high. Brush the aubergine slices with olive oil and grill for 8–10 minutes, turning halfway through cooking, until tender and golden brown.

Place a bowl on the board and spoon in the olives. Arrange the rest of the ingredients on the board and garnish with a few herb sprigs. Serve within 1 hour of assembling.

DOLMAS

Serves 8

1 tbsp olive oil
1 onion, chopped
sea salt and freshly ground black pepper
150g long-grain white rice
50g currants
500ml hot water
50g pine nuts
30g fresh flat-leaf parsley, finely chopped (leaves and stalks)
10g fresh dill, finely chopped (leaves and stalks)
10g fresh mint leaves, finely chopped
1 tsp allspice
½ tsp ground cinnamon
1 tbsp tomato purée
freshly squeezed juice of 1 lemon
16–24 vine leaves, drained

Warm olive oil in a pan over a low heat. Add the chopped onion. Season with salt and pepper and fry for 10 minutes, stirring often, or until the onion is soft but not coloured. Stir every so often.

Stir the rice and currants into the pan. Pour in 350ml hot water and put the lid back on the pan. Turn up the heat and bring to the boil, then turn the heat right down and simmer for 10–12 minutes until the rice is cooked and all the water has been absorbed.

Meanwhile, toast the pine nuts in a dry frying pan for 2–3 minutes until the nuts are golden and smell nutty. Tip into a bowl. Finely chop all the herbs.

Add the pine nuts to the rice with the chopped herbs, spices, tomato purée, and lemon juice. Stir together. Taste and add salt and pepper, if you think it needs it.

Place a vine leaf, stem-side up, on your work surface. Place 1 tablespoon of the filling in the middle of the leaf. Fold the stem up over the filling. Fold the sides over the middle. Take the bottom of the dolma and roll until you reach the tip of the vine leaf. Put to one side. Carry on until you have used up all the filling. How many dolmas you make will depend on how big the vine leaves are.

Nestle the dolmas in a wide, heavy-based pan. Pour in the remaining 150ml hot water and pop on a lid. Cook over a medium–low heat for 25–30 minutes, or until the water has simmered off. These are best served warm or cold rather than piping hot from the pan.

Nachos Platter

A nacho party is the perfect opportunity to bring out a grazing board. Nachos are a natural sharing dish, and you can build your board around your favourite mix of toppings. This platter has a plate of spicy beef nachos as its centrepiece, with side dishes of pickles and sauces to add pops of bright colour and flavour. You can swap in dishes of grated cheese, guacamole, shredded lettuce, soffritas, beans, and hot sauce, or include all those dishes and supersize the nachos to create a giant nacho table. Just scale up the recipe to suit the number of guests, then sanitize a table and cover it in foil. Arrange your nachos and toppings straight on the table to create a massive nacho bar that everyone will love dipping into. Beer and tequila optional, but recommended.

Serves 4

300g Nacho Cheese Sauce (see overleaf)
1 tbsp olive oil
225g beef mince
½–1 tsp chilli powder, to taste
½ tsp garlic granules
1 tsp ground cumin
½ tsp ground coriander
1 tsp dried thyme
a pinch of sea salt
300g tortilla chips
200ml soured cream
200g pico de gallo salsa
140g pickled jalapeño chillies
120g pink pickled red onions

Make the cheese sauce following the recipe on the following page.

Put a frying pan over a high heat and add the oil. Add the beef and fry for 5–6 minutes, stirring often to break up any lumps, until the beef has started to brown. Scoop the beef to one side of the pan, then add the spices (using as much chilli powder as you prefer) and dried thyme, and stir a few times in the hot pan until they smell aromatic. Stir the spices into the beef with a pinch of salt and cook, stirring, for 1 minute. Taste and add more of the spices or salt, if you think it needs it.

Reheat the cheese sauce, if needed. Arrange the tortilla chips on a serving board, layering them with the fried beef. Spoon over half the hot cheese sauce and drizzle over the soured cream. Serve straight away, with the remaining nacho cheese sauce, the salsa, pickled jalapeños, and pickled red onions on the side.

NACHO CHEESE SAUCE

Makes 300g

150g mature Cheddar cheese, coarsely grated
2 tsp cornflour
200ml evaporated milk
2 tsp hot sauce, such as Frank's RedHot®

Combine the grated Cheddar and cornflour in a pan, tossing them together to coat the cheese.

Set the pan over a medium heat. Pour in the evaporated milk and hot sauce and warm, stirring constantly, for 3–5 minutes until the cheese has melted and formed a smooth sauce.

Use straight away, or set aside in a heatproof bowl and reheat in the microwave for 20–30 seconds. The cheese sauce will keep covered for up to 24 hours in the fridge.

Flavour swaps: For a smoother, milder sauce, use a mix of Cheddar and Monterey Jack cheese. If you'd like a spicier sauce, use a combination of Cheddar and Pepper Jack cheese (or Mexicana Cheddar or other spiced cheese).

Spanish Tapas Tasting Board

One of the original ways to graze, Spanish tapas is a well-established way to share lots of delicious little dishes with friends. It's a convivial way to eat, ensuring you get to try lots of tasty bites with everyone participating equally in the feast. This board takes its cue from that tradition and features Spain's most famous cheese and charcuterie, along with salty snacks and freshly cooked Padrón peppers. One of the cured meats I've suggested you feature is Salchichón de Vic, a Spanish salami that's made in the Vic Valley in Catalonia, an area of Spain that's long been known for charcuterie. It's made very simply from pork shoulder and belly with salt and peppercorns. If you can't find Salchichón de Vic, then any good, robust salami will do.

Serves 4

200g olives, drained
400g Manchego
300g whole Salchichón de Vic
200g chorizo, thinly sliced
200g almonds
100g tarallini
100g mini breadsticks
a small bunch of grapes
400g Padrón peppers (see right)
1 loaf of crusty bread, sliced
olive oil to dip (optional)

Place a bowl on your board for the olives, then spoon them in. Cut a few slices from the Manchego and Salchichón de Vic, then arrange them on the board, along with the chorizo. Fill in the gaps with the almonds, tarallini, mini breadsticks, and grapes.

Cook the Padrón peppers, following the recipe opposite. Pop them in a bowl and serve alongside the board, with the sliced bread on the side. Serve as soon as the Padrón peppers are cooked, but you can assemble the rest of the board up to 1 hour ahead.

HOW TO COOK PADRÓN PEPPERS

Padrón peppers are cooked and eaten whole. Most of them are mild, but every so often you'll bite into a pepper and discover that it's fiery hot – playing pepper roulette is all part of the fun.

To cook them, set a frying pan over a high heat and get it very hot. In a bowl, drizzle the peppers with a little olive oil and toss to coat them lightly. When the pan is hot, add the peppers and fry for 3–5 minutes, tossing the pan regularly to turn them, until the peppers have softened, started to wrinkle, and are a little charred in places.

Season with flaky sea salt, then transfer to a serving dish and serve straight away.

Chic Charcuterie & Fromage Board

One for the protein lovers, this grazing board is centred around an elegant selection of European cured meats and cheeses. There are two French cheeses and one Italian cheese, including a Crottin de Chavignol – a soft goat's cheese from the Loire Valley in France. If your local fromagerie doesn't stock it, ask for a creamy goat's cheese with a good, strong flavour. This is a cheese that has to hold its own against pungent Italian Taleggio and earthy Camembert. This combination of meats and cheeses is very rich, which makes it a great board for a buffet or for a games night, when people will want to slowly pick at the food as the evening unrolls. Don't skimp on the pickles or olives, and have a jar of chutney on standby, too (turn to page 162 for a Spiced Plum Chutney).

Serves 6

48 Olive Oil Crackers (see right)
24 Grissini (see page 86 or use ready-made)
2 × 150-g petit Camemberts
200g Taleggio
60g Crottin de Chavignol
12 slices each prosciutto di Parma and bresaola
24 slices salami Napoli
200g whole saucisson sec, sliced
200g mini salami, such as cacciatore salami
190-g jar cornichons, drained
250g green olives, drained
90g caper berries, drained
150g each almonds and pistachios
60g wholegrain mustard
fresh thyme sprigs, to garnish

Make the olive oil crackers following the recipe opposite. If you're making the grissini, follow the recipe on page 86.

Arrange the cheeses on your board, then arrange the charcuterie on the board. Fill in the gaps with the cornichons, olives, caper berries, nuts. Spoon the mustard into a serving dish. Garnish the board with thyme sprigs. Serve within 1 hour of assembling.

OLIVE OIL CRACKERS
Makes 32

275g plain flour, plus extra for dusting
1 tsp baking powder
a pinch of sea salt
45ml olive oil
1 egg white, whisked (optional)
1 tbsp dried thyme or sesame seeds (optional)

2 large baking trays, lined

Sift the flour and baking powder into a mixing bowl. Add a generous pinch of salt and whisk to combine.

Pour the olive oil and 110ml water into the flour. Stir together to make a stiff dough, adding extra water if too dry. Turn out onto your work surface and knead together. Wrap in beeswax paper or cling film and chill for at least 1 hour or overnight.

Preheat the oven to 200°C/Fan 180°C/Gas 6.

Take the cracker dough out of the fridge 15 minutes before you want to roll it out. Dust your work surface with a little flour, then roll the dough out until it's approximately 5 mm thick. Stamp out crackers using a cutter and transfer them to the lined baking tray. Reroll the dough and stamp out more crackers. You should be able to make around 32 crackers, depending on the size of your cutter.

Brush the crackers with the egg white to glaze (optional and leave it out if you want to keep them vegan). Sprinkle over some dried thyme or sesame seeds, if liked. Bake the crackers for 8–10 minutes until golden brown. Transfer to a wire rack to cool. The crackers will keep in an airtight container for 2–3 days.

Fast Food Favourites

Whether it's movie night, games night, or you're just having a fun Saturday night in with the kids and want to treat them to all their favourites, this feasting board is bound to be a hit. It's loaded with every fried food we're told we shouldn't eat, and it's all the more fun for it. Making your own mozzarella sticks is easy, especially if you have an air fryer. If you don't, you can make them in the oven, alongside the fries and nuggets. For the sticks, you need to use mozzarella cucina – a firm, dry mozzarella sold in blocks that's perfect for slicing and cooking. I know no one is likely to eat the salad garnish, but include it on the board. It adds colour and you never know when someone might be tempted by a lettuce leaf.

Serves 4

18 Mozzarella Sticks (see right)
400g French fries
400g potato wedges
12 onion rings
16 chicken nuggets
150g ketchup
150g barbecue sauce
100g sour cream dip
a handful of lettuce leaves
a handful of cherry tomatoes

Make the mozzarella sticks following the recipe right. Cook the French fries, potato wedges, onion rings, and chicken nuggets following the packet instructions.

Arrange some bowls on your board and fill them with the sauces, then arrange the fries and potato wedges in mini fryer baskets or bowls. Arrange the salad garnish on the plate, and then load the board up with the mozzarella sticks, fries, wedges, onion rings, and nuggets.

MOZZARELLA STICKS

Makes 18

400g mozzarella cucina
60g plain flour
1 tsp garlic granules
1 tsp dried thyme
½ tsp smoked paprika
2 medium eggs
sea salt and freshly ground black pepper
80g natural breadcrumbs
oil cooking spray

baking tray, lined

Slice the mozzarella across the block to create nine square slices approximately 1 cm thick. Slice each of these into two fingers.

Tip the flour onto a plate and add the spices. Stir to mix. Crack the egg into a shallow bowl and beat with salt and pepper. Tip the breadcrumbs onto a separate plate.

Roll the mozzarella fingers in the spiced flour and egg twice to completely coat them, then roll them in breadcrumbs to coat. Arrange on the lined baking tray and freeze overnight.

To cook, mist your air-fryer basket with oil and set it to 200°C. Arrange a single layer of the sticks in the basket and air-fry for 8 minutes until golden brown. Transfer to a heatproof plate and keep warm in your oven, set to its lowest temperature. Repeat until you have cooked all the mozzarella sticks. Serve straight away.

Oven-baked: If you don't have an air fryer, you can bake the frozen mozzarella sticks in the oven. Preheat the oven to 200°C/ Fan 180°C/Gas 6. Line a baking tray with foil and mist it with oil. Arrange the frozen mozzarella sticks on the tray and bake for 6 minutes until golden brown.

BBQ Board

Having friends over for a barbecue is one of the joys of summer, but sometimes you don't want to hold too big an event. This sharing board is ideal for when you just want a couple of friends to drop by for an evening of good food, cold drinks, and hot gossip. The chicken wings can be roasted in the oven, before being finished on the barbecue alongside the lamb chops. Make sure there's plenty of barbecue sauce for dunking, butter on standby for the sweetcorn, and napkins for everybody. This is a board that really embodies the concept of finger food, so be prepared to get messy.

Serves 4

1kg Hot Wings (see page 122)
600g Pickled Cabbage Slaw (see right)
1kg new potatoes
4 lamb chops
2 corn on the cob, blanched and quartered
100g baby plum tomatoes
250g barbecue sauce
a few handfuls of salad leaves
a drizzle of olive oil
a drizzle of white wine vinegar
fresh rosemary sprigs, to garnish

Make the hot wings following the recipe on page 122, but finishing the wings on the barbecue. Make the pickled cabbage slaw following the recipe right. Roast the new potatoes. Grill the lamb chops and corn on the cob on your barbecue.

While the food is cooking, pop a couple of bowls on your board and add the slaw, most of the tomatoes, and the barbecue sauce to them. Dress the salad leaves with a little olive oil and vinegar and arrange them on the board. Slice the remaining tomatoes and add to the leaves.

Arrange the chicken wings, lamb chops, corn on the cob, and potatoes on the board. Garnish with rosemary sprigs and serve.

PICKLED CABBAGE SLAW

Makes 600g

450g white cabbage, shredded
1 onion, thinly sliced
250ml cider vinegar
75g caster sugar
½ tbsp fine salt
1 tbsp black mustard seeds
1 tbsp caraway seeds
2–3 fresh dill sprigs

Place the cabbage and onion in a large heatproof bowl. Pour the vinegar and 75ml water into a pan and add the sugar, salt, black mustard seeds, and caraway seeds. Set over a high heat and bring to the boil. When it's boiling, take it off the heat and pour over the cabbage. Stir to mix well, then set aside for at least 1 hour, or overnight.

Pick the soft fronds off the dill sprigs and roughly chop them. When the cabbage has soaked in the pickle brine, drain off the pickling liquid and stir in the chopped dill. Serve straight away.

Meze Collection

If you have a good Middle Eastern delicatessen near you, then putting together a grazing board that's bursting with flavour and colour is extra easy. You could buy everything you need for this board from a food hall, and no one would be sad that you did. Middle Eastern delis laden with huge containers of marinated olives, sun-dried tomatoes, and dolmades, as well as shelves of fresh fruit and veg, and racks of freshly baked bread are a treasure trove of ready-to-eat dishes and gorgeous ingredients. This board is a great opportunity to go shopping and make the most of food-loving local shops. Making your own houmous is easy, and means you can tailor it to your own tastes or add flavours. But ready-made would still be delicious.

Serves 4

300g Houmous (see overleaf)
150g Beetroot Houmous (see overleaf)
150g Turmeric Houmous (see overleaf)
8 Creamy Cheese-stuffed Cherry Peppers
    (see page 167 or use ready-made)
8 falafels
300g tabbouleh
150g sun-dried tomatoes in oil, drained
200g olives, drained
1 fig, quartered
4 pickled peppers, drained
¼ pomegranate
4 large khobez breads, quartered

Make one batch of the houmous following the recipe overleaf, then make a second batch of the houmous, split it in half, and add the beetroot and turmeric to make two flavoured houmous. If you're making the stuffed peppers, use the recipe on page 167. If you're heating the falafel, preheat the oven to 180°C/Fan 160°C/Gas 4 and heat them for 10–15 minutes until hot all the way through.

Place a couple of bowls on the board and spoon in the beetroot and turmeric houmous. Spoon the plain houmous in a big mound on the board. Add the cherry peppers, tabbouleh, sun-dried tomatoes, and olives to the board. Add the fig, pickled peppers, and pomegranate.

You can reheat the bread by placing on a microwaveproof plate lined with kitchen paper and heating on high for 15 seconds. Add the bread to the board along with the warm falafel. Serve as soon as the falafel and bread are ready. You can assemble the rest of the board up to 30 minutes before serving.

HOUMOUS

Makes 300g

400-g tin chickpeas
2 tbsp tahini
2 tbsp extra virgin olive oil, plus extra to drizzle
2 tbsp freshly squeezed lemon juice
1 fat garlic clove, crushed
1 tsp ground cumin
a pinch of sea salt

Set a sieve over a mixing bowl and drain the chickpeas into it, making sure you catch the liquid from the tin. Set aside.

Add the tahini, olive oil, lemon juice, and garlic to a food processor and whizz until combined.

Add half the chickpeas with the cumin and a pinch of salt and whizz until blended. Add the remaining chickpeas with 2 tablespoons of the chickpea liquid and whizz again. If the houmous seems too thick, add another 1–2 tablespoons of the chickpea liquid. Taste the houmous and add more salt, lemon juice, or cumin, if you think it needs it.

To serve, drizzle over a little extra olive oil. The houmous will keep for 2–3 days in a sealed container in the fridge.

Beetroot: Coarsely grate 50g cooked and peeled beetroot, then add it to 150g houmous in the processor. Whizz until combined, adding extra chickpea water if it seems too thick. Taste and adjust the seasoning. This houmous is nice with a pinch of caraway seeds sprinkled over it before serving.

Turmeric: Spoon 150g houmous into a mixing bowl and add ½ teaspoon ground turmeric. Stir well to mix.

Hot Wings Sharing Plate

This grazing plate would make a good starter for four people or a cosy meal for two. It's messy finger food, so you will need to supply plenty of napkins, and only eat it with friends who don't mind seeing each other coated in hot sauce and Thousand Island dip. The Hot Wings are baked, rather than fried, which makes life simple. You can bake the fries on the oven shelf underneath them and easily have everything cooked and ready to eat at the same time.

Serves 2–4

Hot Wings and Thousand Island dip
  (see overleaf)
450g French fries
1 red onion, thinly sliced
½ cucumber, thinly sliced
125g baby plum tomatoes
fresh parsley sprigs, to garnish

Make the wings and Thousand Island dip following the recipe overleaf. Cook the French fries.

While the wings and fries cook, place a bowl on the board and fill with the Thousand Island dip.

When the wings and fries are ready, transfer them to the board straight from the oven. Fill in the gaps with the red onion, cucumber, and tomatoes. Garnish with parsley sprigs and serve straight away.

Make ahead: The Thousand Island dip can be made up to 24 hours ahead, and stored in a sealed container in the fridge. You can also prepare the chicken wings and coat them in the dry spice mix, then marinate overnight in a sealed container in the fridge, ready to cook the next day.

HOT WINGS WITH THOUSAND ISLAND DIP

Serves 2–4

For the wings:
1kg chicken wings
1 tsp garlic granules
½ tsp celery salt
1 tsp cayenne pepper
1 tsp caster sugar
2 tbsp rapeseed oil
75g butter
125ml hot sauce, such as Frank's RedHot®

baking tray, lined with foil

For the Thousand Island dip:
250g mayonnaise
75g tomato ketchup
30ml sweet pickle brine
½ tsp sweet paprika
¼ onion, grated
a pinch of sea salt

Take a chicken wing and turn it over so it's skin-side down and you can easily see the joint. Use your fingers to find the first joint between the drumette and wingette, then use a sharp knife to slice through it. Move down the wing and find the joint between the wingette and the tip. Slice through that. Repeat with all the wings. Discard the wing tips (or you can use them to make stock). Use a small, sharp knife to slash each side of the wingettes and drumettes. Pop them in a large mixing bowl.

In a separate bowl, mix together the garlic granules, celery salt, cayenne, sugar, and oil. Pour over the wings and rub the spice mix into them, making sure they're all coated. Set aside to marinate for 30 minutes at room temperature or overnight in the fridge.

Preheat the oven to 200°C/Fan 180°C/Gas 6. Spread the wings out on the lined baking tray and roast for 45 minutes until the wings are cooked through and browned.

While the wings cook, melt the butter in a small pan. Take off the heat and add the hot sauce. Stir to mix and set aside.

To make the Thousand Island dip, spoon the mayonnaise and ketchup into a bowl and add the pickle brine, paprika, grated onion and a pinch of salt. Mix well, then taste and add a little more salt or brine, if you think it needs it. Spoon into a serving bowl.

When the wings are cooked through, take them out of the oven. Turn the oven up to 220°C/Fan 200°C/Gas 7. Turn the wings over and brush them with the buttery hot sauce, then flip them back over so they're skin-side up. Brush them with more sauce, keeping back 3–4 tablespoons for later.

When the oven is hot, return the wings and roast for a final 10–15 minutes until they're crisp and lightly charred. Remove from the oven and brush with the remaining hot sauce. Serve with the Thousand Island dip and plenty of napkins.

Holidays & Occasions

Game Day Board

Whether it's the Super Bowl, the World Cup, or the Olympics, when there's a big match on, it's fun to have friends round to watch the action and eat snacks. Normally sports snacks go heavy on chips and dips, and that is a good combo that's hard to beat. But it's also nice to mix things up, and swapping in some crunchy veggie crudités can add an extra layer of flavour and colour to your snack tray. Serving them with an indulgently rich French onion dip, made with slowly caramelized onions, and a warm nacho cheese sauce will make sure everyone's taste buds and tummies are satisfied. Add a side of tortilla chips and the hot wings from page 122, and your watch party is good to go.

Serves 10

600g French Onion Dip (see right)
600g Nacho Cheese Sauce (see page 108)
5 medium eggs
1 cucumber, trimmed and sliced into batons
6 sticks celery
3 red peppers
200g baby plum tomatoes
200g sugar snap peas
200g baby carrots
1–2 long red chillies, diced, to taste

Make the French onion dip following the recipe right. If you're making the cheese sauce, follow the recipe on page 108 and make double. Hard-boil the eggs following the technique on page 78.

Prepare the crudités: Trim the ends of the celery sticks, slice each stick into thirds and then into batons. Halve the peppers and scoop out the seeds and white pith. Slice into batons.

Place two bowls on your grazing board for the sauces, then arrange all the veg on the board. Spoon the sauces into the bowls, reheating the cheese sauce if necessary (it's best to serve half the nacho cheese sauce to begin with, then warm up the remainder and refill the bowl as necessary). Top the cheese sauce with the diced chilli. Serve straight away.

FRENCH ONION DIP

Makes 600g

2 tbsp unsalted butter
2 onions, chopped
sea salt and freshly ground
    black pepper
300g cream cheese
200g soured cream
75g mayonnaise
1 tsp garlic granules
1 tsp celery salt
½ tsp cayenne pepper
1 tsp Worcestershire sauce
2 tbsp finely chopped chives

Melt the butter in a frying pan, then add the onions. Season with a pinch of salt and pepper and turn the heat down to very low. Fry, stirring occasionally, for 30 minutes until the onions are well browned and sticky. Don't let them dry out and catch while they fry. Keep the heat low, and if the pan seems too dry add an extra tablespoon of butter and a splash of water. Remove from the heat and set aside to cool.

To make the dip, combine the cream cheese, soured cream, and mayonnaise in a large mixing bowl and beat until smooth. Scoop in the fried onions and add the garlic granules, celery salt, cayenne, and Worcestershire sauce. Stir to mix, taste, and add more celery salt or cayenne if you think it needs it. The dip can either be transferred to a serving bowl straight away, or rested overnight in the fridge to let the flavours mature.

To serve, garnish with the chopped chives.

Big Night-in Board

Whether you're planning a movie night, a board games get-together, cards session, or a Dungeons & Dragons adventure party, you're going to need something to nibble on. This low-effort grazing board is made up of a crispy and crunchy mix of sweet and savoury snacks, including freshly cooked popcorn coated in a homemade maple toffee sauce, hot wasabi peas, and two types of pretzel. It's really easy to put together and will keep the munchies at bay while you get stuck into a *Lord of the Rings* marathon or an epic game of Risk. Use a mix of bowls to create different heights, and think about where you want to arrange those bowls. Creating a snacking station with plates that people can load up is a good idea if table space is at a premium. But if you want everyone to be able to stay in their seats while a movie plays, then arranging the snacks on a low table people can reach from the sofa will keep disturbances to a minimum.

Serves 6–8

200g Maple Toffee Popcorn (see right)
200g plain popcorn
250g cheese savouries
200g wasabi peas
300g tortilla chips
300g salted potato crisps
150g mini pretzels
100g garlic croutons
100g cheese and garlic bread crisps
70g onion rings crisps
70g pretzel sticks

Make the maple toffee popcorn following the recipe right. Make the plain popcorn, following the packet instructions.

Arrange a collection of bowls on your table or board and fill them up with the snacks. Serve within 1 hour of the bowls being filled.

MAPLE TOFFEE POPCORN

Serves 6

2 tbsp unsalted butter
2 tbsp rapeseed oil
150g popping corn
a pinch of sea salt

For the maple toffee sauce:
100g light muscovado sugar
100g unsalted butter
100ml maple syrup
a pinch of sea salt

Heat the butter and oil together in a large pan set over a medium heat, swirling them round until they've melted. Add the popcorn kernels and a pinch of salt. Cover the pan with a lid. The corn should start popping after about 1 minute. When the popping starts to slow down, so there's a 5-second gap between pops, take the pan off the heat. Leave the lid on to catch any last popping kernels.

For the sauce, add the muscovado sugar, butter, and maple syrup to a separate pan with 1 tablespoon water and a pinch of salt. Set over a medium heat and warm, stirring constantly, until the sugar has dissolved. Turn the heat up and bring to the boil, then turn the heat down a little and let the sauce bubble for 2–3 minutes until it's a rich brown colour.

Pour the maple toffee sauce over the popcorn and gently stir to mix. Let it cool for a few minutes, then transfer to a bowl and serve.

All You Need is Cheese Valentine's Day Board

Nothing says 'I love you' like cheese. Lots and lots of cheese. This Valentine's Day-themed board would provide a feast for two cheese fiends (with plenty of leftovers), but it may be even better suited to a Galetintine's get-together, served with glasses of pink fizz and a side of gossip. Heart-shaped truckles of Cheddar normally appear in shops a few weeks before the 14 February. Another heart-shaped cheese to look out for is Neufchâtel, a bloomy semi-soft cheese that dairymaids have been making in France for their loved ones since the 14th century. If your local stops don't stock cheesy hearts, cut slices from your favourite cheese then stamp out hearts using pastry cutters.

Serves 4

10–12 Paprika & Parmesan Hearts (see right)
3 salami roses (see page 28)
200g petit Brie de Meaux
2 × 200-g Cheddar hearts
36 mixed savoury crackers
4 slices prosciutto di Parma
a handful of almonds
a small bunch of grapes
a handful of strawberries
4 macarons
4 chocolate truffles
fresh sage leaves, to garnish

Make the paprika and Parmesan hearts following the recipe right. Make the salami roses, following the instructions on page 28, using 8–12 slices of salami per rose.

Place the cheeses on the board, then arrange the paprika and Parmesan hearts, crackers, salami roses, prosciutto di Parma, almonds, grapes, and strawberries around them. Tuck the macarons and truffles onto the board. Garnish with sage leaves. Serve within 1 hour of being made.

PAPRIKA & PARMESAN HEARTS
Makes 10–12 hearts

50g plain flour
½ tsp sweet paprika
a pinch of sea salt
50g cold butter, diced
50g Parmesan, finely grated
1 tbsp full-fat milk

baking tray, lined
heart-shaped pastry cutter

Sift the flour and paprika into a mixing bowl and add a pinch of salt. Whisk together to combine. Tip them into a food processor.

Add the butter and whizz until the mixture resembles breadcrumbs. Add the grated Parmesan and milk. Whizz again to bring the dough together. Turn out the dough and gently squeeze it into a ball. Wrap in cling film or beeswax paper and chill for at least 30 minutes, or overnight.

Preheat the oven to 200°C/Fan 180°C/Gas 6.

Take the dough out of the fridge and let it sit at room temperature for 10–15 minutes to soften a little. Dust your work surface with flour and roll the dough out until 5 mm thick. This dough is very short, so it will be crumbly to start with. Be firm but gentle with it and it will roll out. Stamp out crackers using the heart-shaped cutter and transfer them to the baking tray with a palette knife – they will be sticky. Reroll the trimmings and stamp out more. You should have 10–12 hearts.

Bake for 10–15 minutes until a pale golden brown. Transfer to a wire rack to cool completely. The hearts will keep for 3–4 days in an airtight tin.

Sweets for My Sweetie Valentine's Board

For many people, the idea of heading to a crowded restaurant on Valentine's Day is a quick way to crush any romantic feelings that might be starting to stir. Instead, stay at home and seduce that special someone with a grazing board generously laden for two. This grazing platter is a tempting mix of sweet berries, chocolates, and homemade biscotti, along with cute cheese hearts, slices of salami, and melt-in-the-mouth crackers. It's fun to share – whether you feed just yourself or each other is up to you – and it can be easily assembled in under 15 minutes. Just prep the cheese hearts and keep them in the fridge, ready to go on the board. Then take your time getting ready before quickly assembling the platter. That way both you and dinner will look completely irresistible.

Serves 2

8 Vanilla Biscotti (see right)
200g mature Cheddar
50g raspberries
80g blackberries
12 crackers
12 slices salami Milano
50g pecans
4 raspberry jam biscuits
12 chocolate hearts
75g strawberries

heart-shaped pastry cutter

Make the vanilla biscotti following the recipe right. Stamp hearts out of the Cheddar using the heart-shaped cutter.

Place a bowl on the board and fill it with raspberries and blackberries. Arrange the crackers and salami on the board, then fill in the gaps with the pecans, biscuits or biscotti, chocolate hearts, and strawberries. Serve within 1 hour of the board being assembled.

VANILLA BISCOTTI

Makes 24

200g plain flour
200g caster sugar
½ tsp baking powder
a pinch of sea salt
1 medium egg
2 tsp vanilla extract
1–2 tbsp milk, as needed

large baking tray, lined

Preheat the oven to 180°C/Fan 160°C/Gas 4.

Sift the flour into a large mixing bowl, then add the sugar, baking powder, and a pinch of salt. Whisk together to mix.

In a separate bowl, beat the egg and vanilla together. Pour into the dry ingredients and stir with a fork to bring the dough together. If it's a bit dry, add 1–2 tablespoons milk, as needed.

Turn the dough out onto your work surface, lightly knead together, then slice it in half. Shape each half into a log around 25 × 10 cm. Transfer to the lined tray and bake for 40–45 minutes until golden brown.

Remove the biscotti logs from the oven and let cool for a few minutes. Transfer to a chopping board and use a serrated knife to slice each log into individual biscotto, around 2 cm thick.

Place the biscotti back on the tray (lining an extra tray with baking paper if there's not enough room on your original tray). Bake for 10–15 minutes until dry and crisp-looking. Transfer to a wire rack to cool. The biscotti will keep in an airtight tin for 1–2 weeks.

St Patrick's Day Party Platter

If you're celebrating all things Irish on 17th March, then this green grazing board is perfect for your party. The stars of the show should be the homemade cupcakes and vibrant emerald avocado dip, but it's probably the Irish cheeseboard that will steal everybody's heart. I've picked four big-hitters from the world of Irish cheese and you can build your board around them. There's a good farmhouse Cheddar (shamrock-shaped or otherwise), buttery and rich Cashel Blue, bloomy St Killian semi-soft cheese, and a mild and bright St Tola goat's cheese log, which you buy plain or lightly coated in ash. Other Irish cheeses to look out for include peppery Crozier Blue, sharp and tangy Bellingham Blue, mature farmhouse Coolea, and the earthy-tasting Gubbeen and Durrus.

Serves 6

6 Green & White Vanilla Cupcakes (see overleaf)
300g Avocado, Pea & Cannellini Dip (see page 194)
45 mixed savoury crackers (or make shamrock-shaped Paprika & Parmesan crackers, see page 30)
3 green peppers
350g shamrock-shaped Cheddar
200g Cashel Blue cheese
150g St Killian cheese
200g St Tola goat's cheese log
300g olives or cornichons
crinkle-cut gherkins, drained
12 slices prosciutto di Parma
12 slices jamon Iberico
12 slices salami Napoli
3 kiwi fruit, halved
2 green apples or pears, cored and sliced
a bunch of green grapes
1 cucumber, thinly sliced

shamrock cutter

Make the cupcakes following the recipe overleaf. Make the avocado, pea, and cannellini bean dip following the recipe on page 194. If you'd like to make shamrock-shaped crackers, use the recipe for paprika and Parmesan hearts on page 130 and stamp out the crackers with a shamrock cutter. You can also stamp shamrocks out of the green peppers – halve the peppers, remove the seeds and white pith, then stamp out the shamrocks.

Arrange the cheeses on your grazing board or table, then place bowls on the board and fill them with the avocado, pea, and cannellini bean dip, olives, and gherkins. Add the cupcakes, then arrange the hams, salami, fruit, crackers, peppers, and cucumber on the board. Serve within 1 hour of being assembled.

GREEN & WHITE CUPCAKES

Makes 6

350g unsalted butter, softened
125g caster sugar
2 medium eggs
1 tsp vanilla extract
125g self-raising flour
a few drops of green food colouring
350g icing sugar
green and yellow sprinkles (optional)

6-hole cupcake tin, lined with paper cases

Preheat the oven to 180°C/Fan 160°C/Gas 4.

Measure out 125g of the butter and pop into a mixing bowl. Add the sugar and beat together with electric beaters until pale and fluffy.

Beat the eggs in a separate bowl with the vanilla extract, then add half to the butter and sugar mix. Beat to combine. Add 1 tablespoon flour and fold that in. Add the remaining eggs and beat until combined. Add the remaining flour and fold together. If you'd like to dye the cakes green, add a few drops of green food colouring and fold it in.

Spoon the batter into the cake cases. Bake in the preheated oven for 20–25 minutes until the cakes are risen and springy to the touch. Remove from the oven and transfer to a wire rack to cool completely.

To make the icing, add the remaining 225g butter to a mixing bowl and beat with electric beaters until smooth and creamy. Add half the icing sugar and gently beat until combined. Add the remaining icing sugar and beat again. Scoop half the buttercream icing into a separate bowl and add a few drops of green food colouring. Stir to mix.

Fit a piping bag with a 1M or 2D nozzle (large rose- or star-shaped nozzle). Spoon the vanilla icing down one side of the bag and then spoon the green icing down the other side. Twist the top of the bag to seal, then squeeze the icing until the two colours are coming out together, creating a two-tone mix. Pipe the icing on top of the cupcakes. Top with sprinkles and serve. The cupcakes will keep for 1–2 days in an airtight tin.

Spring has Sprung Celebration Board

As the weather warms up, spring festivals begin to appear on the calendar. Easter, Passover, Ramadan, Holi, and New Year celebrations across Asia and the Middle East are all celebrated just as the sun begins to return to the Northern Hemisphere. It's a wonderful time of year to get together and celebrate fresh starts and new beginnings. This colourful board includes some symbols commonly associated with Easter – eggs, bunnies, and carrots – and combines them with some crowd-pleasing cheese and charcuterie, alongside a handful of fresh fruit and veg. It's a light, bright board that is simple to put together and would be delicious eaten in the garden on the first warm day of spring.

Serves 6

6 Carrot Arancini (see page 139)
4 medium eggs
6 mini tortillas
6 Bruschette Toasts (see page 89 or use
   ready-made)
200g petit Brie de Meaux
1 ball mozzarella
1 tbsp fresh chopped parsley leaves
1 tbsp chopped hazelnuts
1 tbsp chopped cooked beetroot
12 crackers
6 slices cooked ham
6 slices bresaola
6 slices salami Milano
1 apple, cored and sliced
a handful of radishes, trimmed and sliced
a handful of strawberries
a handful of grapes
fresh parsley sprigs and edible flowers,
   to garnish

rabbit-shaped pastry cutter

Make the carrot arancini following the recipe on page 139. Cook, peel, and halve the eggs following the instructions on page 78. Stamp rabbit shapes out of the mini tortillas using the rabbit-shaped cutter. If you're making your own bruschette toasts, follow the recipe on page 89.

Place the Brie and mozzarella on the board. Top the mozzarella with the chopped parsley, chopped hazelnuts, and chopped beetroot.

Add the arancini, tortillas, toasts, eggs, and crackers to the board, then fill in the gaps with the cured meats, fresh fruit, and radishes. Decorate the board with a couple of parsley sprigs and edible flowers. The arancini should be served hot, so serve this board as soon as it's assembled.

CARROT ARANCINI

Makes 6

1 tbsp olive oil
1 tbsp unsalted butter
1 small onion, chopped
100g carrot, coarsely grated
sea salt and freshly ground black pepper
1 garlic clove, crushed
1 tbsp fresh thyme leaves
150g risotto rice
100ml dry white wine
500ml vegetable or chicken stock
75g Parmesan, finely grated
75g mozzarella, chopped into 6 pieces
100g plain flour
2 medium eggs
125g natural breadcrumbs
1 litre sunflower oil, for deep-frying
sprig of curly leaf parsley, to garnish

Warm the olive oil and butter in a pan over a medium heat. When the butter has melted, add the onion and carrot and season with salt and pepper. Gently fry, stirring often, for 8 minutes, or until glossy and starting to soften.

Add the garlic and thyme to the pan and cook, stirring, for 1 minute, or until aromatic. Add the rice and cook, stirring, for 3–4 minutes until the rice has started to look pearly at the edges. Turn the heat down to medium–low. Pour in the wine and cook, stirring, for 3–4 minutes until the wine has been absorbed.

Add all the stock to the rice and stir well to mix. Pop a lid on the pan and simmer for 20 minutes, stirring occasionally, until the rice is tender. Take the pan off the heat and stir in the Parmesan. Let the risotto cool, then transfer to a container and chill overnight in the fridge.

To make the arancini, divide the cooled rice into six rounds. Flatten one round in the palm of your hand and place a piece of mozzarella in the middle. Wrap the rice around the mozzarella to cover it. Repeat to use up the remaining mozzarella.

Tip the flour onto a plate and season with salt and pepper. Crack the eggs into a shallow bowl and beat together. Tip the breadcrumbs onto a third plate. One at a time, roll the arancini in the flour, then the egg and then the breadcrumbs to coat them. Once coated, transfer to a baking tray. Chill them for at least 1 hour, or overnight.

To cook the arancini, heat the sunflower oil in a deep-fryer or pan to 170°C. Cook 2–3 arancini at a time in the hot oil, turning them occasionally, for 8–10 minutes, or until golden brown all over. Lift out of the oil with a slotted spoon and drain on a plate lined with kitchen paper. Serve warm.

Shape shifting: To turn your arancini into 'carrots' for your grazing board, shape them into a cone rather than a ball before you egg, flour and breadcrumb them. Once cooked, push a sprig of curly leaf parsley into the bigger end of each arancino to mimic carrot leaves.

Red, White & Blue Board

Dessert grazing boards always draw a crowd back to the table, even if everyone says they're full from dinner. No one can resist eating something sweet, especially when it's beautifully displayed. This tricoloured board would be a huge hit at 4th July parties, or any other occasion when a mix of red, white, and blue matches the occasion. This board is particularly brilliant for two reasons. Firstly, you can make it hours in advance and then keep it somewhere cool and dry, lightly covered with mesh nets or beeswax paper, ready to serve. Secondly, because there's as much fresh fruit on the board as there are sweets, chocolate, and biscuits, which means the board is full of colour and fresh flavours, as well as indulgent, sugary treats.

Serves 8–10

350g red sweets, such as liquorice twists, jelly lips, cinnamon balls, and peppermints
350g blue sweets, such as bonbons, foam sweets, and mints
350g red fruit, such as raspberries and strawberries
a large bunch of red grapes
350g blue fruit, such as blueberries and blackberries
200g white chocolate
100g white chocolate fingers
90g white chocolate wafers

Place three bowls on your serving board and add some red, white, and blue sweets to each bowl.

Arrange the rest of the fruit, sweets, chocolate, and biscuits on the board, loading the left-hand side of the board with red items, the middle with white, and the right-hand side of the board with blue items. Serve within 4–6 hours of being assembled (keep the board covered until you're ready to serve).

HOW TO CREATE A THEMED BOARD

In theory, you can put together any grazing board and it will always be well received at your party. Everyone can appreciate and enjoy a beautifully presented mix of cheese, charcuterie, crudités, fruit, and snacks. But if you match your board to your party, the plaudits will be doubled. There are several ways you can theme your board.

Cuisine: If you're celebrating a national day, like Independence Day, or an event that's specific to a particular country or region, such as Bastille Day, then it makes sense to match the food to the country. Make national dishes the focus of the board and try to source other snacks and ingredients from that region, too.

Time: You can match the food to the time of day. While cheese and charcuterie can be snacked on at all hours, making breakfast foods the focus of morning boards, and sandwiches, scones, and cakes the heart of afternoon party boards, will help ground your party in the moment.

Colour: Red, white, and blue is a colour combination that works for several national days and saints days around the world, and the mix of three colours looks fabulous. For a baby shower, you might offer a mix of pink and blue dishes, or pink, blue, and white. At Christmas, green and red foods feel festive, while in the spring, use a mix of pastels to create a soft, sunny vibe.

Flavours: The usual rule is to offer a balanced mix of sweet, salt, savoury, and spice, but that doesn't mean you can't major on one or two ingredients to create impact. In the autumn, go big on apples and pears by turning them into chutneys, pies, and cakes, as well as serving them freshly sliced to go alongside cheeses and cured meats.

Halloween Candy Board

Halloween means trick or treating, and that can happen inside your house as well as out. So if you're holding a Halloween party, dot some sweetie-loaded dessert boards around the room and your guests can help themselves to as many treats as they like, without resorting to any tricks. This sharing board will serve 4–8 people, depending on how big they – and their appetites – are. It's a great opportunity to bring out any Halloween dishes and decorations you have, as well as an opportunity to get creative and turn innocent, harmless-looking breadsticks into truly terrifying witches' fingers.

Serves 4–8

4 Chocolate-dipped Breadsticks (see right)
4 Witches Fingers (see right)
100g Maple Toffee Popcorn (see page 129 or use ready-made)
450g mixed Halloween sweets, including chocolate eyeballs, strawberry liquorice, jelly worms, chocolate pumpkins, and foam sweets
100g mini pretzels

Make the chocolate-dipped breadsticks and witches' fingers following the recipes on the right. If you want to make your own toffee popcorn, follow the recipe on page 129.

Place a couple of bowls on your grazing board and fill them with some of the popcorn and sweets. Arrange the chocolate-dipped breadsticks and witches' fingers on the board, then fill in the gaps with the pretzels and the rest of the sweets. Add spooky decorations and serve within 2–3 hours of being assembled. Keep the board covered with mesh nets or beeswax paper until you're ready to serve.

CHOCOLATE-DIPPED BREADSTICKS

Makes 8

150g milk chocolate
60g orange and black sprinkles
8 breadsticks

baking tray, lined

Chop the chocolate into small chunks and melt it in the microwave on high, checking and stirring it every 10 seconds until it's melted and smooth. (Alternatively, place the chopped chocolate in a heatproof bowl and set it over a pan half-filled with simmering water. Take the pan off the heat and don't let the water touch the bowl, as that will overheat the chocolate. Sat over the hot water, the chocolate should melt within 5–10 minutes.)

Scoop the sprinkles into a mug or bowl.

Dip a breadstick into the chocolate to coat half of it, then dip it into the sprinkles. Place on the lined baking tray. Repeat until you've used up all the breadsticks, chocolate, and sprinkles. Chill the breadsticks in the fridge for 1–2 hours to set. These are best eaten within 24 hours.

Witches' Fingers: To turn your chocolate-dipped breadsticks into witches' fingers, use white chocolate and dye it green with food colouring. Dip the breadsticks into the green chocolate, then press a flaked almond on the end of each breadstick to make a fingernail. Chill to set.

Hanukkah Party Board

This midwinter festival of light is a good excuse to put away the grazing board and bring out the grazing table. If you're celebrating with friends and family, then sharing a spread of hearty dishes is the perfect way to mark the occasion and share the joy that this time of year can bring, even if the nights are long and dark. This grazing table is laden with Jewish favourites, including sweet and sour braised brisket and noodle kugel. Potato latkes served with apple sauce are non-negotiable and the other must-haves are jam-filled sufganiyot. All you need to add are dreidels, twinkling lights, and loved ones to honour the feast.

Serves 10

3.5kg sweet and sour braised brisket, sliced
1kg noodle kugel
32 Potato Latkes (see right)
800g challah bread
450g apple sauce
450g chopped liver
10 sufganiyot
8 sticks celery, chopped into thirds
6 large carrots, peeled and chopped into batons

If you're making the brisket and noodle kugel, make them well ahead of your gathering and keep them warm. Alternatively, if you have sourced them from a deli, reheat them following the instructions.

Make the potato latkes following the recipe on the right.

Place the challah bread on your grazing table, then add bowls of apple sauce and chopped liver. Arrange the sufganiyot on a plate and add to the table. Add the warm brisket, arranging the celery and carrots around it, and add a dish for the sauce. Add the kugel and the potato latkes to the table and serve straight away.

POTATO LATKES

Makes 32

2kg potatoes, such as Desiree, peeled
2 onions
4 medium eggs
sea salt and freshly ground black pepper
olive or rapeseed oil, for frying

Finely grate the potatoes. If you have a food processor, use the grating attachment to speed this up and save your fingers.

Tip the potatoes into a large mixing bowl and cover with cold water. Swirl round until the water goes cloudy, then drain and return to the bowl. Cover with fresh water, swirl, and drain again. Washing the potatoes like this helps get rid of the starch.

Tip the potatoes into a large sieve and squeeze as much water out as possible. If you don't have a large sieve, tip the potatoes into a muslin cloth and wring it to squeeze out the water. Leave the potatoes in the sieve, or in a muslin-lined colander, set over a bowl, to drain off any remaining water.

Coarsely grate the onions. Crack the eggs into a large bowl and whisk them with a pinch of salt and pepper. Add the onions and stir to mix. Add the potatoes and stir again to combine.

Put a plate in your oven and set it to its lowest temperature. Place a large, heavy-based frying pan over a medium heat and warm it for a few minutes. Lightly coat the pan with oil and add tablespoons of the latke mix to the pan, allowing 1 heaped tablespoon per latke. Flatten the latkes with the back of your spatula and fry for 2–3 minutes until golden brown underneath. Flip them over and fry for a further 2–3 minutes.

Take the plate out of the oven and line it with kitchen paper. Transfer the latkes to the plate and keep warm in the oven while you use up all the latke mixture. Serve straight away.

Holiday Snack Wreath

If you're looking for a fun way to serve canapés at your festive get-togethers, then this charcuterie wreath could be exactly what you're after. The skewers look gorgeous but they're very easy to put together and you can assemble them a few hours before the party. Just keep them covered and chilled, then fetch the wreath out of the fridge 30 minutes before you want to serve. This platter allows two skewers per person, and assumes you'll be serving other nibbles. If you want to have an all-skewer party, allow three skewers per person per hour and mix and match the ingredients. A range of skewers – including savoury charcuterie, fresh veggies, and sweet fruit – will keep everyone interested in trying just one more bite.

Serves 4–8

2 red peppers, deseeded, cut into 2-cm squares
150g Taleggio rind removed and cut into
    10 equal-sized chunks
10 baby plum tomatoes
10 black olives, pitted
10 bocconcini, drained
10 slices salami Napoli
a few handfuls of curly green kale
fresh rosemary and basil sprigs, to garnish

Assemble the skewers, threading a piece of red pepper, a cube of Taleggio, a tomato, an olive, a bocconcino, and a slice of salami onto each skewer. You don't have to make the skewers uniform, so mix up the order in which you add ingredients to the skewers.

Arrange a few handfuls of curly green kale leaves in a doughnut shape on a serving board or plate. Nestle the skewers on the leaves, using the leaves as cups to support the skewers. Tuck in a few sprigs of rosemary and basil to garnish.

If your fridge is big enough, lightly cover this board with cling film or beeswax paper and store in the fridge for 3–4 hours. Take it out of the fridge 30 minutes before serving.

FLAVOUR SWAPS

These skewers are incredibly versatile, and make a great trick to have up your sleeve for parties throughout the year. This wreath uses Italian ingredients, but you can pick and choose from your favourite flavours. Here are some ideas.

Make it French: Sliced saucisson sec, jambon de Bayonne, cubed Roquefort, sliced Comté, and cornichons

Make it Greek: Cubed feta, sliced cucumber, cherry tomatoes, pitted Kalamata olives, and grilled red onion wedges

Make it veggie: Artichoke hearts, grilled peppers, basil leaves, sliced mozzarella, and cherry tomatoes

Make it vegan: Cubed marinated tofu, grilled tempeh slices, grilled aubergine slices, and baby spinach leaves

Make it fruity: Blackberries, dried apricots, grapes, prosciutto di Parma, and bocconcini

Make it sweet: Sliced bananas, strawberries, marshmallows, cubes of fudge, and pineapple chunks

Make it breakfast: Cubed croissants, strawberries, and cubed Fontina cheese

Christmas Cookie Grazing Board

The quickest way to create a cosy atmosphere during the holiday season is to have a good supply of festive snacks on hand to welcome any guests who happen to drop by. This cookie board is perfect for that midwinter period when friends and family may turn up at your door, ready to share some Christmas cheer. The board is simple to put together, and including some homemade gingerbread biscuits will make it extra impressive. It can stay on your sideboard for hours, ready for hungry visitors. It also makes a stunning sweet centrepiece for festive get-togethers, carol concerts, and gift exchanges. If you have a garden and can light a fire, then combining this board with the hot chocolate from page 170 makes for a very festive spread that will keep you warm and well-fed while you gather round and celebrate in the firelight.

Serves 12

24 Gingerbread Biscuits (see overleaf)
300g peppermint sweets
400g hazelnut and cocoa wafer rolls
12 sugar cookies
12 double chocolate chip cookies
12 chocolate-covered cookies

Make the gingerbread biscuits following the recipe overleaf.

Place a dish in the centre of the grazing board and add the peppermint sweets to it. Arrange the gingerbread biscuits, wafers, and cookies on the plate. Serve within 2–3 hours of assembling.

GINGERBREAD BISCUITS

Makes 30–60

150g unsalted butter, diced
75ml maple syrup
400g plain flour, plus extra for dusting
1 tsp bicarbonate of soda
100g light muscovado sugar
1 tbsp ground ginger
1 tsp ground cinnamon
a pinch of sea salt
1 medium egg
1–2 tbsp full-fat milk, as needed

4 large baking trays, lined
festive pastry cutters of your choosing

Place the butter and syrup in a pan and melt over a low heat, stirring to combine. Set aside to cool.

Sift the flour and bicarbonate of soda into a large mixing bowl. Add the sugar, ginger, and cinnamon with a generous pinch of salt. Whisk the dry ingredients together to mix them.

Crack the egg into a separate bowl and beat it. Add the egg and melted butter mixture to the dry ingredients. Stir together to make a soft dough. If it seems a little dry, add 1–2 tablespoons milk.

Turn the dough out onto a work surface and knead gently to bring it together. Wrap in beeswax paper or cling film and chill for 1 hour or overnight.

Take the dough out of the fridge 45 minutes before you want to bake the biscuits. Preheat the oven to 180°C/Fan 160°C/Gas 4.

Dust your work surface with a little flour and divide the dough into quarters. Lightly knead one of the quarters to soften it, then roll out the dough until it's around 5 mm thick. Stamp out biscuits using the cutters and transfer them to the lined baking trays. Don't overcrowd the trays – leave a 5-cm gap in-between the biscuits – bake the biscuits in batches if necessary.

Repeat, re-rolling the trimmings until you have cut out all your biscuits (or bake and roll biscuits as you go). You should make 30–60 biscuits, depending on the size of your cutter.

Bake each tray of biscuits for 10–12 minutes until browned and crisp. Transfer to a wire rack to cool. The biscuits will keep for up to 3 days in an airtight tin.

Christmas Candy Snack Tray

A few savoury snacks have snuck their way onto this grazing board to help balance out the sugar, but mostly this board is a delicious celebration of all things sweet. It's perfect for a Christmas coffee or festive afternoon tea with friends and family, when you want to make sure your guests feel welcome but don't want to create too much work for yourself. Too many of us get stuck in the kitchen and miss out on the celebrations during the festive season. Instead, shop for some sweet treats, add a couple of homemade elements, and that way you get to sit down and enjoy the gathering rather than spending all your time on the catering. If you make one thing for this platter, bake the fruitcake. You can make it a week before you want to serve it, as long as you feed it some brandy (or whisky, rum, port, or sherry). In fact, it will keep for months, as long as it's well-wrapped in paper and foil and fed once a week with some liquor. If you're used to dry, crumbly fruitcakes, then this homemade version will be a revelation.

Serves 12

1 Festive Fruitcake, sliced (see overleaf)

12 Choc Chip Cookies (see page 174)

a large bunch of red grapes

24 crackers, such as Ritz, mini breadsticks, or other

400g hazelnut and cocoa wafer rolls

100g mini marshmallows

6 peppermint candies

6 glazed ring doughnuts

600g mixed sweets, such as chocolate M&Ms, bonbons, fizzy laces, jelly beans, jelly sweets, and candy hearts

100g hazelnuts

2 oranges, sliced

Make the festive fruitcake following the recipe overleaf. If you're making the choc chip cookies, follow the recipe on page 174.

Slice the fruitcake and arrange it on your grazing board. Place the grapes on the board, then start arranging the other elements so they fan out around the board. Leave the orange slices off the board, adding them just before you serve. Without the orange slices, the board can sit for 2–3 hours somewhere cool and dry.

FESTIVE FRUITCAKE

Serves 12

125g unsalted butter, plus extra for greasing
180g light muscovado sugar
400g mixed dried fruit, such as raisins, currants,
   or dried cranberries
100g glacé cherries
50g candied angelica or mixed peel, chopped
225g plain flour
1 tsp ground cinnamon
2 tsp mixed spice
2 medium eggs
2–3 tbsp brandy (optional, plus extra for feeding)

*900g loaf tin, greased and lined, making sure the paper comes
3 cm above the top of the tin*

Chop the butter and add to a pan. Tip in the sugar and pour in 225ml water. Set over a medium heat and gently warm, stirring, until the butter has melted. Add the mixed dried fruit and bring to a gentle boil. Simmer for 10 minutes, stirring occasionally, until the fruit is soft and the mixture is syrupy. Take off the heat and stir in the cherries and angelica/mixed peel. Set aside to cool completely (overnight is best).

Preheat the oven to 160°C/Fan 140°C/Gas 3.

Sift the flour into a large mixing bowl. Add the spices and whisk to combine the dry ingredients. Crack the eggs into a separate bowl and beat.

Add the soaked fruit and their liquid to the dry ingredients and pour in the beaten eggs. Use a flexible spatula to fold the ingredients together. Scrape the mix into the prepared cake tin. Bake for 2 hours–2 hours 30 minutes, or until the cake is risen, firm, and a skewer inserted into the middle comes out clean. Check the cake after 60 minutes; if the top is dark brown, lightly cover it with a sheet of baking paper to slow down the browning.

Take the cake out of the oven and poke a few holes in the top of the cake with a skewer. Pour over the brandy, if using, then let the cake cool in the tin. Transfer to an airtight tin. The cake will keep for up to 7 days in the tin. If you want to keep it for longer, wrap it in baking paper and then a layer of foil. Once a week, unwrap it and pour 1–2 tablespoons brandy over the cake to feed it. Rewrap tightly and keep in the tin. It should keep for several months while you feed it, becoming rich and moist.

New Year's Eve Party Platter

The best thing about throwing a party in December is how easy it is, thanks to all the ready-made canapés you can find in the shops. The supermarket chiller cabinets are laden with mini tarts, filo parcels, tiny pies, satay sticks, spring rolls, and miniature versions of fancy foods like beef Wellington and chicken Kyiv – all perfect for catering a party. For hosts who love a low-effort spread, it's the best time of year. If you want a way to elevate those ready-made nibbles, incorporate them into a grazing table. They add crunch and flavour, while all the different elements you get on a grazing board make the buffet look even more impressive. Prepare any homemade elements, like the toasts or grissini the day before. Decorate the cookies and Brie wedges in the afternoon, keeping the cookies in a tin and the Brie wedges in the fridge. Two people should be able to put this table together in under 30 minutes, so when you want to put the food out, grab a friend, get the canapés and baked Brie in the oven, and then build the rest of the dishes while the finger foods heat up. As soon as everything is out of the oven, call everyone to the table to tuck in before the New Year arrives.

Serves 8–10

24 Bruschette Toasts (see page 89 or use ready-made)
24 Grissini (see page 86 or use ready-made)
12 sugar cookies
fondant icing
200g petit Brie de Meaux
black food colouring
12 slices prosciutto di Parma
24 slices chorizo
24 slices salami Napoli
2 apples, sliced
150g walnut halves
150g almonds
200g stuffed olives, drained
200g black olives, drained
450g salted potato crisps
48 crackers
1 prawn ring with ketchup
48-piece baked canapé collection
200g Baked Brie with Maple Pecans (see opposite)

If you're making the bruschette toasts, follow the recipe on page 89. To make the grissini, follow the recipe on page 86. Either make sugar cookies, or buy plain cookies and then use fondant icing to make clock faces to decorate them. Slice the mini Brie into wedges and use black food colouring to decorate them so they look like tuxedos.

Arrange the bruschette toasts, grissini, cookies, and Brie wedges on platters. Add the cured meats and sliced apple. Fill bowls with the nuts, olives, and crisps. Add crackers to the platters along with the prawn ring.

Heat your canapé selection according to the packet instructions. Make the baked Brie following the recipe opposite.

When the canapés and baked Brie are ready, add them to the grazing table and serve straight away.

BAKED BRIE WITH MAPLE PECANS

Serves 6

200g petit Brie de Meaux
75g pecan halves
3 tbsp Demerara sugar
3 tbsp honey
a pinch of sea salt

Preheat the oven to 180°C/Fan 160°C/Gas 4. Unwrap your Brie and place it in a snug baking dish. Bake the Brie in the oven for 15–20 minutes until soft and gooey-looking.

Meanwhile, toast the pecans in a dry frying pan, shaking the pan regularly, until they're browned and smell nutty. Add the sugar and honey to the pan with a pinch of salt. Gently warm, stirring occasionally, for 3–4 minutes or until the sugar has dissolved to form a sauce. Take off the heat.

Take the Brie out of the oven. Spoon over the honeyed pecans and serve straight away.

Indulgent

Meat Lover's Platter

The ultimate no-effort board is a charcuterie board that is focused on cured meats and only on cured meats. This board is heaven for anyone who loves eating salamis and hams from around the world, whether they're air-dried, salt-cured, or cooked. Throughout this book I often say that you can experiment with the ingredients on your board and swap in flavours you prefer. This is especially true for this board, which is best designed around the charcuterie that you love. Choose a mix of hams, salamis, and cured meats, making sure there's a range of spices and textures. If you're not ready to design your own board just yet, this selection will make a great starting point.

Serves 6

300g olives, drained
200g whole saucisson sec
200g mini salami, such as cacciatore salami,
    petits saucissons secs, or mini kabanos
12 slices prosciutto di Parma
12 slices chorizo
12 slices salami Milano
12 slices soppressata (or other dry pork salami)
a handful of cherry tomatoes
fresh rosemary sprigs, to garnish
1 loaf of ciabatta, sliced, to serve after sliced

Place a bowl on your board and spoon in the olives. Slice half the saucisson sec. Place the remaining whole saucisson sec on the board, and then arrange the mini salami on the board.

Add the sliced saucisson, the prosciutto, chorizo, salami, soppressata, and the tomatoes to the board. You can lightly cover the board with cling film or beeswax paper and keep it in the fridge for 2–3 hours, if you have space.

If the board has been in the fridge, take it out and let it sit at room temperature for 30 minutes. Garnish with rosemary sprigs and serve with ciabatta on the side. If you're not chilling it, serve within 30 minutes of being assembled.

DRINK-CHARCUTERIE PAIRINGS

Matching charcuterie with drinks can be tricky. Charcuterie is often very rich, and it can be heavily spiced, peppery, or garlicky. These are strong flavours, which can be hard to match to a drink by themselves, and if you have a board with all of them on it, then it can seem impossible. But there are options.

Champagne: Everything goes with Champagne. A glass of well-chilled sparkling wine is a good all-rounder because the acidity will cut through the meats' fattiness. Look for dry Champagnes that have citrusy notes and hints of crisp apple in their flavour profile.

Lambrusco: If you don't like a sparkling white, try a sparkling red. In Emilia-Romagna effervescent Lambrusco wines are often paired with pork. Seek out bottles of dry Lambrusco Salamino, a frothy red wine with refreshing berry flavours.

Beaujolais: When you have a lot of spicy salamis on your charcuterie board, go for a bottle of this light French red. It's a mellow wine with plenty of juicy fruitiness and mellow tannins that won't clash with the meats' aromatics.

Sour beers: Tangy sour beers are a great match with charcuterie. Their acidity stands up to the fat, while the gentle fizz keeps your mouth lively and your palate refreshed.

Amaros: Bitter Italian amaros are often served in bars during aperitivo hour alongside salty snacks, so it's no surprise that they go well with cured meats. Campari and soda, Americano, negroni, and the all-conquering Aperol spritz all make a great choice if you're looking for cocktails to serve alongside your grazing board.

Fresh Seafood Platter

An indulgent mini platter for two, this luxurious grazing board is all about enjoying the best the sea has to offer. The star of the board will undoubtedly be the lobster. Find a fishmonger who will cook the seafood for you and who you trust to find you good, fresh oysters. Keep everything on ice at home until you're ready to serve, and crack open the oysters at the last minute (use an oyster knife or a butter knife to prise the shells apart, and wrap your hands in a tea towel to protect them). If you're making your own mayonnaise, remember that it uses raw egg yolks, so it shouldn't be served to young children, the elderly, or anyone with a compromised immune system. You can find cartons of pasteurized egg yolks, which would make it safer to eat if you have concerns. Use around 40g pasteurized egg yolk in place of 2 raw egg yolks.

Serves 2

8 tbsp Mayonnaise (see right)
4 tbsp Marie Rose Sauce (see right)
a handful of chives, finely chopped
2 tbsp white wine vinegar
½ shallot, finely chopped
400g whole cooked lobster, halved
4 oysters
8 cooked mussels
2 cooked prawns
2 cooked crayfish
1 lemon, sliced into wedges
1 lime, sliced into wedges

Make the mayonnaise and Marie Rose sauce following the recipes right. Divide the mayonnaise between two small bowls and top one bowl with the chopped chives. Spoon the Marie Rose sauce into a third bowl. In a fourth bowl, mix the vinegar and finely chopped shallot.

Place the bowls on a serving plate, then arrange the seafood around it. Add the lemon and lime wedges. Serve straight away.

MAYONNAISE

Makes 250g

2 egg yolks
½ tsp each sea salt and Dijon mustard
2 tsp white wine vinegar
230ml rapeseed oil

Place the egg yolks in a clean, grease-free, non-plastic bowl, then add the salt, mustard, and vinegar. Whisk together to combine. Trickle in the oil, around 1 teaspoon at a time, and whisk between each addition. Once you've added half the oil, you can start speeding up the oil, adding around 1 tablespoon at a time. When all the oil has been added and you have a rich, creamy mayonnaise, taste and add a pinch more salt or a little more mustard, if you think it needs it. Transfer to a container, seal, and store in the fridge for up to 3 days.

MARIE ROSE SAUCE

Makes 100g

100g Mayonnaise (see above)
1 tbsp tomato ketchup
¼ tsp each Worcestershire sauce and hot sauce,
   such as Tabasco
½ tsp lemon juice
1 tsp brandy (optional)
sea salt and freshly ground black pepper

Spoon the mayonnaise into a mixing bowl, then add the remaining ingredients and season with a pinch of salt and pepper. Stir together to make a smooth, pink sauce. Taste and add more salt, pepper, lemon juice, or hot sauce, if you think it needs it. Transfer to a container, seal, and store in the fridge for up to 3 days.

Decadent Cheese Board

Cheese lovers will adore this grazing board. It's loaded with a gorgeous range of cheeses from across Europe, all chicly matched with a mix of condiments and side dishes in complementary shades of black, red, and purple. Arranging these ingredients on a black slate helps to emphasize the creamy whites and yellows of the cheese. Because the sides tone with the slate, they blend into the background, making the cheeses stand out even more. It's a fab way to really draw attention to the cheese, and when the cheeses are as delicious as these, they deserve to have the spotlight.

Serves 6

250g Spiced Plum Chutney (see right)
250g olives, drained
120ml clear honey
200g petit Camembert
200g petit Brie de Meaux
200g mature Cheddar
150g Parmesan
150g Saint Agur blue cheese
150g young Gouda
150g aged Gouda
100g Crottin de Chavignol
150g walnuts
2 bunches of red and/or black grapes
72 crackers

Make the spiced plum chutney following the recipe right.

Place bowls on your serving board and fill them with the chutney, olives, and honey.

Arrange the cheese on the board, slicing some of them and leaving others whole to create an interesting mix of shapes. Add the walnuts, grapes, and crackers to the board. Serve within 1 hour of being assembled.

SPICED PLUM CHUTNEY

Makes 1.2kg

900g plums, stoned and roughly chopped
2 red onions, finely chopped
2 apples, peeled and coarsely grated
6-cm piece of fresh ginger, peeled and grated
1 tbsp black mustard seeds
1 tbsp cumin seeds
1 tbsp sweet paprika
2 tsp dried chilli flakes
400ml red wine vinegar
400g Demerara sugar
2 tsp sea salt

Place the plums, red onions, apples, ginger, and spices in a large pan. Pour in the red wine vinegar. Set over a high heat and bring to the boil. Turn the heat down a little and simmer for 10 minutes, stirring occasionally, until the plums are soft.

Stir the sugar and salt into the plums. Keep simmering the chutney for 30–45 minutes, stirring often to stop it catching and burning, until the chutney has reduced by about a third. Spoon the chutney into sterilized jars (see page 81) and seal. The sealed chutney will keep for approximately 6 months in a dry, dark cupboard.

Moody Blues Board

Sometimes, we're so used to how things are normally done that we forget that there are different ways to approach things. This riff on a cheeseboard focuses on just one cheese, a pungent wedge of blue cheese, and pairs it with a refreshing mix of sweet, juicy fruits. The fruits don't just complement the cheese's flavour, they match it tonally as well. The blend of colours creates a stunning visual effect, which lifts the cheeseboard and turns something familiar into an exciting and chic experience. I've used Roquefort in this board but, as ever, you can hero your favourite blue cheese. This is a great board to serve at the end of a meal with friends. Or, if you want to make an impression on someone special, serve it as a light meal with chilled glasses of Sauternes.

Serves 4

6 figs
300g Roquefort
a bunch of black grapes
200g blackberries
100g raspberries
16 savoury crackers

Slice 3 of the figs in half. Arrange the Roquefort cheese and grapes on a board. Add the figs to the board, then fill in the gaps with the blackberries, raspberries, and crackers. Serve within 1 hour of being assembled.

AROUND THE WORLD IN BLUE CHEESE

Roquefort is one of the most famous blue cheeses ever made. Known as the 'cheese of Kings and Popes' in France, it has an intense, complex flavour that balances the salty white paste with hot veins of blue mould. If you love blue cheese, then Roquefort is probably already one of your favourites. But it's not the only blue cheese worth showcasing on this grazing board. Try some of these blues from across the globe.

Gorgonzola: There are two types of Gorgonzola to choose from. Dolce is aged for 2 months and is soft and creamy with a delicate sour tang, while piccante is matured for at least 3 months and is firmer with an intense, spicy bite.

Stilton: The king of English cheeses, Stilton is a mellow cheese with a velvety texture that melts in the mouth. It has a nuttiness to it that develops into a complex, salty finish. This is milder than Gorgonzola and Roquefort, but no less delicious.

Rogue River Blue: In 2019 this cheese was named World Champion at the World Cheese Awards in Italy, beating over 3,800 other cheeses to the trophy. An organic blue cheese produced in Oregon, it has a luxuriously fruity flavour, which is balanced with an almost meaty saltiness.

Cashel Blue: This Irish farmhouse blue cheese is milky with a chalky texture when young, becoming creamier and more buttery as it ages. Three-month-old Cashel Blues are rounded and rich, with a fuller flavour and a touch of spice.

Sapphire Blue: Known as the Tasmanian Roquefort, this sheep's milk cheese from Australia is a dense semi-soft cheese, marbled with veins of blue. It has a bloomy orange rind and robustly spicy flavour that is said to pair well with both prosecco and dark chocolate. Something to consider when building a grazing board around it.

Cabrales: This artisanal blue cheese is produced in Asturias, northern Spain. It's made with milk from cows that graze in the mountains on the summer pastures, then it's aged in the natural limestone caves in those same mountains. It has a dense, creamy texture and a powerfully spicy flavour.

A Little Bit of Everything

A grazing board for people who want it all, this indulgent platter is a mouthwatering mix of cheeses, cured meats, sweet fruits, and savoury snacks. It's gloriously extravagant and would make a beautiful centrepiece at a family dinner – much more fun to gather around and share than a standard Saturday night dinner. As it's so big, it's best assembled in situ. It will take around 30 minutes to put together, not including the cooking time for any of the dishes, and can sit for around 30–60 minutes. You can lay it out, welcome everyone in and fix drinks, then hit the grazing table for a feast.

Serves 8

18 Creamy Cheese-stuffed Cherry Peppers (see opposite)
8 Grissini (see page 86 or use ready-made)
200g Nuts in Honey Syrup (see page 184)
12 slices prosciutto di Parma
1 pomegranate
300g olives, drained
250g cherry tomatoes
200g Stilton
200g Cheddar or Red Leicester
200g petit Brie de Meaux
250g petit Camembert
200g whole red wine salami
12 picnic salamis
6 slices peppered salami
64 savoury crackers
a handful of walnuts
a few small bunches of grapes
1 large loaf of sourdough bread, sliced

Make the creamy cheese-stuffed cherry peppers following the recipe opposite. If you are making the grissini, follow the recipe on page 86. To make the nuts in honey syrup, follow the recipe on page 184.

Wrap 8 slices of prosciutto di Parma around the 8 grissini. Keep the rest of the prosciutto for the board. Quarter the pomegranate.

Place a few bowls on the board and fill them with the stuffed peppers, nuts in honey syrup, olives, and cherry tomatoes. Add the cheeses to the board, the whole red wine salami, the prosciutto-wrapped grissini, and the remaining prosciutto slices.

Fill in the gaps with the picnic salamis, peppered salami, crackers, walnuts, and grapes. Serve within 1 hour of being assembled with the sliced sourdough.

CREAMY CHEESE-STUFFED CHERRY PEPPERS

Makes 18–20

50g cream cheese
50g feta, crumbled
1 tbsp fresh thyme leaves, roughly chopped
½ tsp garlic granules
1 tsp white wine vinegar
sea salt and freshly ground black pepper
380-g jar hot cherry peppers, drained

In a mixing bowl, combine the cream cheese, feta, thyme, garlic granules, and vinegar. Season with a little salt and pepper then beat to mix well. Taste and adjust the seasoning.

Fill a disposable piping bag with the mixture, snip off the end, and pipe it into the cherry peppers, or use a teaspoon to fill the peppers. Transfer the stuffed peppers to a container, seal, and store in the fridge. They'll keep for up to 3 days.

Sweet & Decadent

Hot Chocolate Tasting Board

One of the best things about the arrival of winter is hot chocolate. You can drink hot chocolate at any time of year and in any weather, if you're determined, but there's something special about drinking a warm and cosy mug of cocoa when the skies outside are dark and the rain, snow, and sleet have started to fall. This hot chocolate board will thrill children and impress the grown-ups. Line up mugs of hot chocolate next to the board, along with snack bowls, and let your guests pick their hot chocolate toppings along with the sweets, wafers, and chocolates they'd like to nibble on. If the weather is clear you can take your drinks outside to enjoy around a fire, or snuggle up indoors with a movie and your treats.

Serves 6–8

2 litres Hot Chocolate (see right)
125g mini marshmallows
75g amaretti biscuits
200g marshmallows
140g hard butterscotch sweets
225g toffees
150g wafer rolls
12 chocolate biscuits
75g peppermint chocolate sticks
100g peppermint honeycomb thins
75g white chocolate, coarsely grated

Make the hot chocolate following the recipe right, and keep it warm in a pan on the hob.

Place a couple of bowls on the board and fill them with mini marshmallows and amaretti biscuits. Fill in the gaps with the marshmallows, butterscotch, toffees, wafer rolls, biscuits, and chocolates.

Ladle the hot chocolate into mugs and let everyone tuck into the grazing board.

HOT CHOCOLATE

Makes 2 litres

8 tbsp cocoa powder
8 tbsp soft brown sugar, plus extra if needed
2 litres milk of your choice
100g dark chocolate (80% cocoa solids),
    roughly chopped

Tip the cocoa powder and sugar into a pan. Add 250ml of the milk and whisk together until smoothly combined. Trickle in the rest of the milk, whisking constantly so no lumps form. Add the chopped chocolate to the pan.

Set the pan over a medium heat and gently warm, whisking occasionally, until it's steaming hot. Gently simmer for 2–3 minutes, whisking regularly. Taste and add more sugar if it needs it. Ladle into warm mugs and serve, letting it cool down a little if you're serving it to children.

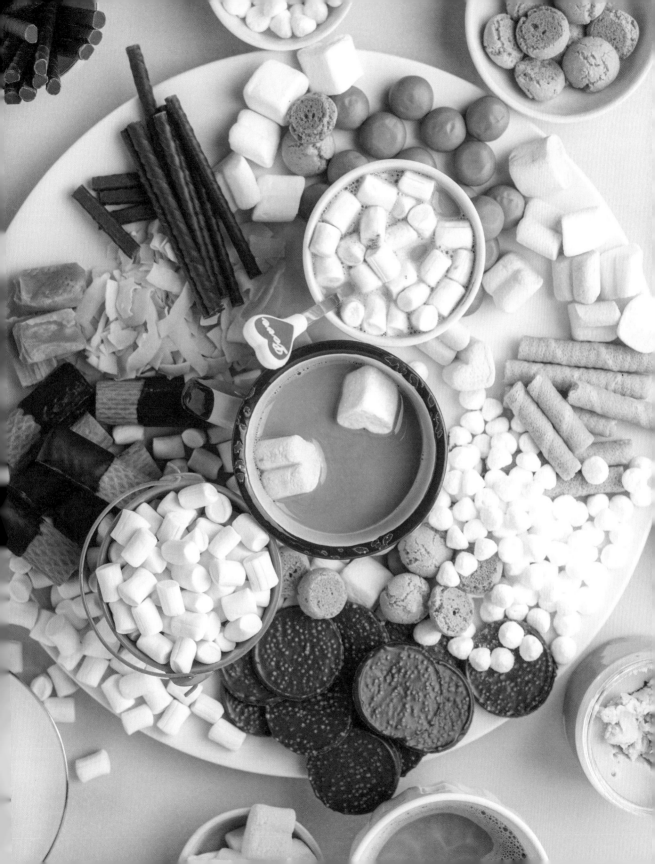

Chocolate Fondue Board

Desserts can sometimes be tricky, whether they're for a dinner party or to go on a buffet. It's easy to get carried away and think you have to bring out something spectacular to finish a meal, but never forget how good a simple chocolate sauce is – especially when it's paired with fresh fruits for dipping. No one can resist dunking a strawberry or chunk of banana into a warm, luxurious chocolate sauce. Using dark chocolate in the fondue adds bitterness to the dish, which helps balance out the fruit's sweetness. But if dark chocolate is a little too rich for your guests, then use a good milk chocolate spiced up with cinnamon, or try making it with white chocolate flavoured with ground cardamom.

Serves 4

1 kiwi fruit, sliced
1 apple, cored and sliced
1 banana, peeled and sliced
1 mango, peeled, stoned, and cubed
100g strawberries
50g raspberries
a small bunch of grapes
300g Salted Chocolate Sauce (see right)
fresh mint leaves, to decorate

Prepare all the fruit. Place a bowl on a grazing board, then arrange the fruit around it.

Make the salted chocolate sauce following the recipe right. Pour the warm sauce into the bowl, decorate with mint sprigs, then serve the board straight away.

SALTED CHOCOLATE SAUCE

Serves 4

100g dark chocolate (85% cocoa solids)
a small pinch of sea salt, plus extra if needed
200ml double cream
50g unsalted butter, chopped

Chop the chocolate into small pieces and place in a heatproof bowl. Add a small pinch of salt.

Pour the cream into a small pan and add the chopped butter. Gently warm for 2–3 minutes until the butter has melted and the cream is steaming hot. Pour the hot cream and butter into the bowl with the chocolate and stir until the chocolate has melted and formed a smooth sauce.

Taste the sauce and add a pinch more salt, if you think it needs it. Pour into a serving dish and serve straight away.

S'Mores Board

Bring your childhood campfires indoors with this nostalgic grazing board. It's perfect for chilly evenings and wet, rainy nights when you can't toast your marshmallows over an open fire. Instead, grill them in a heatproof frying pan and then serve them with this tempting mix of cookies, digestive biscuits, chocolate spread, and peanut butter. You can get creative making up s'mores with a mix of cookies, melted marshmallows, and spreads. Be mindful that the pan will be hot – wrapping the handle in a tea towel can help protect fingers if you get forgetful. On warm evenings, make up the board, but take it outside with the marshmallows in a bowl and a set of skewers. Light a fire and let everyone toast their own marshmallows.

Serves 6

6 Choc Chip Cookies (see right)
150g marshmallows
100g chocolate spread
100g smooth peanut butter
200g milk chocolate
100g white chocolate
12 digestive biscuits
6 chocolate-covered biscuits
60g mini marshmallows

Make the choc chip cookies following the recipe right. Pop the marshmallows into an ovenproof frying pan, saving a few for adding to the board. Preheat the grill to high.

While you wait for the grill to heat up, place a couple of bowls on your board and spoon the chocolate spread and peanut butter into them. Add the blocks of chocolate and all the biscuits to the board, leaving a big gap for the frying pan.

Slide the pan of marshmallows under the grill for 2–3 minutes until golden brown. Place the pan on the board (make sure it's heatproof). Fill in the gaps with the mini marshmallows and the reserved larger marshmallows. Serve, being careful of the hot pan.

CHOC CHIP COOKIES

Makes 12-25 cookies, depending on size

200g plain flour
1 tsp baking powder
a pinch of sea salt
150g unsalted butter, softened
125g Demerara sugar
1 medium egg
100g chocolate chips

2 large baking trays, lined

Sift the flour and baking powder into a mixing bowl and add a pinch of salt. Whisk together.

In a separate bowl, beat the butter and sugar together with electric beaters until fluffy. Beat the egg in a separate bowl and add a little to the butter and sugar mixture. Beat to combine, then add more beaten egg and beat again. Repeat until you've beaten in all the egg.

Add the choc chips and stir to mix them in. Fold in the flour to make a soft dough. Shape it into a log, wrap in cling film or beeswax paper and chill the dough for 12–24 hours.

Preheat the oven to 190°C/Fan 170°C/Gas 5.

Slice a cookie off the log, about 1 cm thick. Place on the tray. Repeat, making sure the cookies are well spaced apart. Bake for 15–20 minutes until golden brown. Transfer to a wire rack to cool completely. The cookies will keep for up to 3 days in an airtight tin.

Make ahead: The cookie dough keeps really well in the freezer for up to 3 months, so you can keep it on hand to slice and bake cookies when you want them. You can bake the cookies from frozen. They will just take a little longer in the oven.

Perfect Pavlova Board

Pavlova is one of the world's favourite desserts. It's so popular that two countries – Australia and New Zealand – argue over who invented it. Food historians like to track back through magazine articles and news reports from both countries, trying to find the first recipe. So far they have turned up dozens of pavlova cakes, meringue tarts, and fruit-and-jelly desserts that all seem to have fed into the creation of the pavlova that we know and love today. And with so much variety in its history, you can enjoy including a range of toppings on this dessert board. Meringue, fruit, and cream are obviously essential. In Australia, peppermint chocolate thins are a must-add item, so make sure you include some chocolate. Crumbling ginger biscuits over the top adds spice and texture, while toasted nuts add crunch.

Serves 8

8 Meringue Nests (see right)
500ml double cream, whipped
1 pomegranate, seeds only
2 peaches, peeled, stoned, and chopped
250g strawberries
300g blueberries
1 mango, hedgehogged (see page 201)
16 ginger cookies
100g milk chocolate, chopped into
   bite-sized chunks
100g mixed nuts, toasted
fresh mint sprigs, to decorate

Make the meringue nests following the recipe right.

Place some bowls on your grazing board and spoon the cream into a large bowl. Add the pomegranate seeds, chopped peaches, strawberries, and blueberries to the remaining bowls. Place the hedgehogged mango directly on the board.

Add the meringue nests to the board. Fill in the gaps with the ginger biscuits, chocolate, and nuts. Decorate with mint sprigs and serve straight away.

MERINGUE NESTS

Makes 8–16

6 medium egg whites
300g caster sugar
1 tsp cornflour
1 tsp white wine vinegar

2 large baking trays, lined

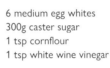

Preheat the oven to 150°C/Fan 130°C/Gas 3.

Pour the egg whites into a large, clean, non-plastic bowl, making sure no yolk gets into the bowl. Whisk them until frothy, then add the sugar 1 tablespoon at a time and whisking between each addition. As the sugar is incorporated, the egg whites will become white, stiff, and glossy. When you've added three-quarters of the sugar, you can begin adding it a few tablespoons at a time.

When the meringue mixture has formed glossy, stiff peaks, add the cornflour and vinegar and fold through with a metal spoon, trying not to knock out too much air.

Spoon the meringue onto the lined baking trays, swirling it to make individual meringue nests. You should be able to make eight palm-sized meringues or 16 smaller nests. Use a piping bag if you want neater-looking nests.

Bake the meringues in the oven for 1 hour, then turn the heat off and leave the meringues to cool in there for a few hours or overnight. When cold, transfer to an airtight tin. The meringue nests will keep for up to a week.

Tasty Four Frosting Boards

The sweet alternative to the butter board (see page 42), the frosting board is a sugar-lover's dream. It starts with a layer of buttercream frosting that you then load up with toppings and serve with biscuits, wafers, or chunks of cake to drag through the mix. If you want to find out more about frosting boards, turn to page 45. If you can't wait to get started, then use this recipe to create your own homemade buttercream, add your preferred flavouring, and then start piling on the toppings. These boards are very sweet, so normally you need to allow just three biscuits or chunks of cake per person to serve alongside the frosting.

All recipes below serve 8

BIRTHDAY CAKE FROSTING

450g Vanilla Buttercream (see overleaf)
1–2 tbsp pomegranate molasses
30g multicoloured sprinkles

Make the buttercream following the recipe on page 181 and then pipe or spoon it onto a serving board or plate, using a palette knife or the back of your spoon to create swirls. Drizzle over a little pomegranate molasses, then scatter over the sprinkles. Serve straight away. You can swirl the buttercream on the board and keep it in the fridge until you're ready to decorate, if you want to prepare it ahead.

COFFEE & WALNUT CAKE FROSTING

450g Coffee Buttercream (see overleaf)
1–2 tbsp clear honey
50g walnuts, finely chopped

Make the buttercream following the recipe on page 181 and then pipe or spoon it onto a serving board or plate, using a palette knife or the back of your spoon to create swirls. Drizzle over a little honey, then scatter over the chopped walnuts. Serve straight away. You can swirl the buttercream on the board and keep it in the fridge until you're ready to decorate, if you want to prepare it ahead.

LEMON DRIZZLE CAKE FROSTING

450g Lemon Buttercream (see below right)
2 tbsp lemon curd
60g blueberries
20g candied mixed peel, finely sliced

Make the buttercream following the recipe right and then pipe or spoon it onto a serving board or plate, using a palette knife or the back of your spoon to create swirls. Warm the lemon curd in a microwave for 10–20 seconds to make it more pourable, then drizzle it over the buttercream. Scatter over the blueberries and sliced mixed peel. Serve straight away. You can swirl the buttercream on the board and keep it in the fridge until you're ready to decorate, if you want to prepare it ahead.

VANILLA BUTTERCREAM FROSTING
Makes 450g

150g unsalted butter, room temperature
300g icing sugar
1–2 tbsp full-fat milk
1 tsp vanilla extract

Scoop the butter into a large mixing bowl and beat until soft and creamy. Sift in half the icing sugar and beat until smooth. Sift in the remaining icing sugar and add 1 tablespoon milk and the vanilla. Beat until smooth. If it seems a little stiff, you can beat in a little more milk. (If you're adding more liquid flavouring, such as with the lemon or coffee buttercream, add that first to see if it loosens the texture.)

Scoop the buttercream onto a plate or board or transfer to a container and chill in the fridge for up to 3 days. Remove from the fridge 15 minutes before you want to use it. You may need to beat it again to loosen the texture after it has been chilled.

Coffee buttercream: Replace the vanilla with 3 teaspoons instant coffee dissolved in 1 teaspoon boiling water.

Lemon buttercream: Replace the vanilla with the finely grated zest and juice of 1 lemon.

Quick & Easy

The Unexpected Guests

In this age of almost constant communication, unexpected guests shouldn't really ever happen – surely everyone knows to message first? – but that doesn't mean spontaneous socializing doesn't occur. Whether it's family members suddenly turning up at your door or a last-minute decision to have friends round, this grazing board will save your hosting bacon. All you need to do to put it together is raid the cheese drawer in your fridge – or the deli counter in your local shop – and arrange the cheeses on a beautiful block. The nuts in honey syrup takes less than 15 minutes to make and they will wow people when they're served alongside the cheeses with crackers and bunches of juicy, fresh grapes.

Serves 6

225g Nuts in Honey Syrup (see right)
150g mixed olives, drained
200g petit Camembert
150g Brie de Meaux
150g Roquefort
150g Gouda
1 pomegranate
a few small bunches of grapes
54 crackers

Make the nuts in honey syrup following the recipe right.

Place a couple of bowls on your grazing board and spoon in the nuts in honey syrup and the olives. Arrange the cheeses on the board, then add the pomegranate, grapes, and crackers. Serve within 30 minutes of being assembled.

NUTS IN HONEY SYRUP

Makes 225g

70g nuts, such as cashews, hazelnuts, or almonds
60g clear honey
15g unsalted butter, chopped
a small pinch of sea salt

Place a frying pan over a medium heat and tip in the nuts. Toast, stirring often, for 2–3 minutes, or, until the nuts smell aromatic and are looking a little browned.

Pour in the honey and add the butter. Gently warm, stirring occasionally, until the honey and butter have melted and formed a sauce. Add a small pinch of salt, then transfer to a serving dish or to a sterilized jar (see page 81), seal, and store in the fridge for up to 1 week.

The In-Laws Are Coming

You've received a WhatsApp that has made your heart sink: unexpected guests are on their way and you know they're going to want something to eat. It doesn't matter if they're in-laws, friends, colleagues, or family, or if they've breezily insisted you don't need to go to any trouble. Hospitality demands they are offered something delicious to snack on, which is where this emergency board comes in. Easily assembled from ingredients you have in your fridge and cupboards, or from a quick trip to the local shop, it's a low-effort but impressive board.

Serves 4

300g Houmous (see page 120 or use
    ready-made)
150g Beetroot Houmous (see page 120 or
    use ready-made)
200g tzatziki
200g mixed olives, drained
200g almonds
75ml clear honey
200g petit Brie de Meaux
200g Cheddar
16 savoury crackers
125g mini breadsticks
6 Grissini (see page 86 or use ready-made)
1 apple, cored and sliced
a handful of strawberries
a bunch of grapes
fresh rosemary and sage sprigs, to garnish

You can make the houmous and beetroot houmous following the recipes on page 120, but if it's an emergency, you'll probably want to use ready-made.

Place a few bowls on your board and spoon in the houmous, tzatziki, olives, almonds, and honey.

Place the Brie and Cheddar on the board. Fill in the gaps·with the rest of the ingredients.. Garnish with rosemary and sage sprigs. Serve within 45 minutes of being assembled.

QUICK TOPPINGS FOR HOUMOUS

Often the only thing houmous needs to top it is a drizzle of extra virgin olive oil. But there are some simple toppings you can make or find in your kitchen cupboards that will elevate a simple bowl of houmous into a seriously stylish treat.

Pine nuts: Toast pine nuts in a dry frying pan for 2–3 minutes until golden brown. Use to top houmous with grated lemon zest, freshly chopped parsley, and a drizzle of olive oil.

Za'atar: A Middle Eastern spice blend made with dried thyme, sumac, toasted sesame seeds, and a pinch of salt, za'atar is a delicious flavour enhancer. Keep a jar in your cupboard and you'll have a ready-made boost for your houmous.

Tapenade: Traditionally made with black olives, tapenade is an umami-rich sauce, which you will find in chiller cabinets in supermarkets. A combination of minced black olives, garlic, capers, anchovies, lemon, and thyme, it's punchy and a few spoonfuls will go a long way.

Habas fritas: These crunchy snacks are made from broad beans that have been fried and lightly salted. They're great for nibbling on, but are even better used as a topping for houmous and other dips, sprinkled over soups, and added to salads. Other fried legumes, like chickpeas, also make great toppings and it's worth having a bag handy in your kitchen.

The Big Cheese

If you want to make a splash without expending too much brainpower or effort, focus on just one ingredient and go really big with it. This board is oriented around cheese, with just a few condiments and sides to complement the flavours. This means that three-quarters of the board is all the same colour and yet instead of looking boring, it looks impressive. I guarantee people's eyes will light up when they spy this grazing platter on your table and they will be thrilled to tuck in. Although there are no crackers on this plate, set up a basket next to it with a range of savoury crackers, digestive biscuits, oatcakes, and crusty bread to complete the look.

Serves 6

12 Grissini (see page 86 or use ready-made)
125ml clear honey
125ml pomegranate molasses
200g Manchego, sliced
200g Cheddar, sliced
200g Gouda, sliced
200g Roquefort, cubed
100g Parmesan, broken into flakes
100g Swiss cheese, cut into shapes
200g petit Brie de Meaux
300g mixed salted nuts
a few small bunches of grapes
a handful of strawberries, sliced

If you're making the grissini, follow the recipe on page 86.

Place a couple of bowls on the board and pour in the honey and pomegranate molasses.

Arrange the cheeses on the board, filling in the gaps with the nuts, grapes, and strawberries. Serve within 1 hour of being assembled.

HOW TO SLICE AND STORE CHEESE

One thing you may have noticed about this board is that a lot of the cheeses have been sliced. The usual rule is to slice cheese as close to serving as possible, but when you're preparing a big platter of cheese it helps to be able to slice and store it ahead of time.

Start by slicing wedges of hard cheese, like Manchego and Cheddar. Use a sharp cook's or utility knife and place the wedge on your chopping board on one of its cut sides. Trim any rinds off the top and bottom of the cheese, then slice through the wedge to create triangle-shaped slices of cheese. Transfer the cut slices to a sheet of greaseproof paper and wrap, then place in a container, seal, and store in the fridge.

Semi-firm cheeses, like Gouda and Swiss, can be sliced and stored in a similar way.

Aged cheeses, like Parmesan, can be broken into flakes by inserting a Parmesan knife or the tip of a cook's or utility knife into the wedge of Parmesan. This will cause the cheese to break into chunks. Transfer to a tub, seal, and store in the fridge.

Soft cheeses, like the Brie or Roquefort are best sliced just before serving.

All the cheese can be stored overnight in the fridge and then brought out 30 minutes before serving.

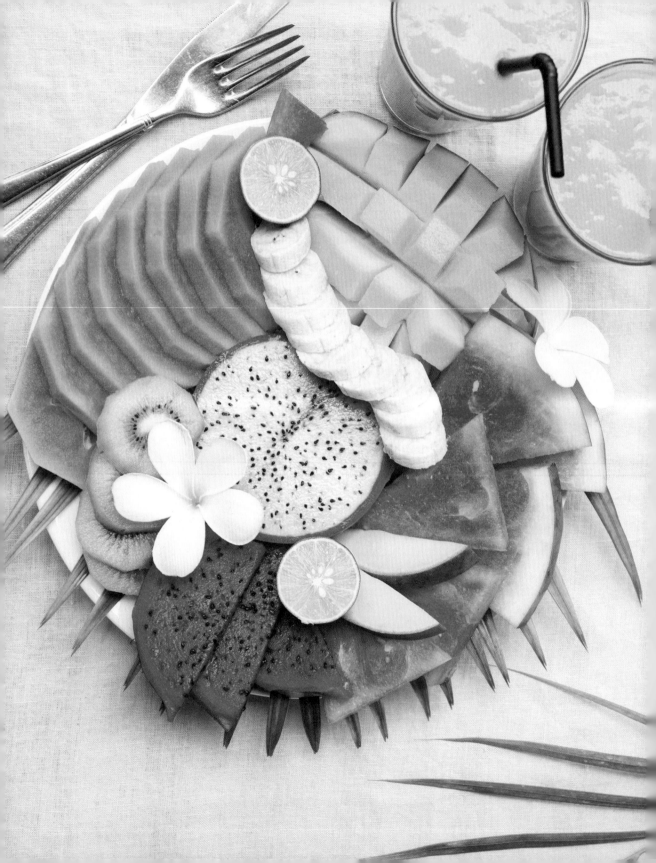

Healthy

Rainbow Fruit & Veg Board

Eating the rainbow is good for us, and beautiful too. An array of vegetable crudités, arranged by colour, looks spectacular on a grazing board, especially when served with vibrantly coloured, freshly made dips. This board is best served soon after being arranged, so get ahead by preparing all your crudités and keeping them in containers in the fridge, ready to go on the board. You can make the dips up to 24 hours in advance, too. Then it's simply a matter of heaping the veggies and chips up on the board in brightly coloured piles and adding the dips. It should take around 15 minutes to assemble, but because the combination of colours has such impact, everyone will imagine you've worked on it for hours (the most satisfying hosting trick). This is a great board for summer parties, or serve it as an appetizer or side at barbecues, where the freshness of the veg will balance the richness of the meat.

Serves 8

600g Avocado, Pea & Cannellini Bean Dip (see overleaf)
300g Houmous (see page 120 or use ready-made)
300g Beetroot Houmous (see page 120 or use ready-made)
16 Grissini (see page 86 or use ready-made)
150g baked pitta chips
150g blue corn tortilla chips
1 cucumber
3 large carrots
6 sweet bite peppers
300g mixed radishes
500g sugar snap peas
150g small broccoli florets
125g baby plum tomatoes
mustard cress, to garnish

Make the avocado, pea and cannellini bean dip following the recipe overleaf. If you're making the houmous and beetroot houmous, follow the recipe on page 120. If you're making your own grissini follow the recipe on page 86.

Place three bowls on your grazing board and fill them with the dips. Arrange the grissini, pitta chips, and tortilla chips on the board.

Trim and slice the cucumber into finger-length batons, Trim, peel, and slice the carrots to match. Halve the sweet bite peppers and scoop out the seeds and white pith. Trim and slice some of the radishes into rounds and slice others into flower shapes, if liked, leaving other radishes whole. Arrange all the veg on the board, strewing some mustard cress across the board to garnish. Serve this board within 30 minutes of being assembled.

AVOCADO, PEA & CANNELLINI BEAN DIP

Makes 600g

200g frozen peas
1 medium avocado
400-g tin cannellini beans
50g mature Cheddar, grated
2 garlic cloves, crushed
1–2 tbsp freshly squeezed lemon juice
1–2 tbsp olive oil
sea salt and freshly ground black pepper

Bring a pan of water to the boil and add the peas. Simmer for 3 minutes to just cook them through, then drain. Halve the avocado, scoop out the stone, and peel away the skin. Roughly chop. Drain the cannellini beans, catching the liquid from the tin in a bowl.

Place the peas, avocado, and beans in a food processor. Add the Cheddar, garlic, and 1 tablespoon each lemon juice and olive oil. Season with a pinch of salt and pepper. Whizz until smoothly combined. Taste the dip and add more salt, pepper, lemon juice, or olive oil, if you think it needs it. If it seems too chunky or too stiff, add a few tablespoons of the reserved liquid from the cannellini bean tin.

Spoon the dip into a serving bowl. The dip will keep for up to 24 hours in a sealed container in the fridge. Cover the top of the dip with a thin layer of olive oil to help prevent it browning, and stir that in before serving.

Wholesome Vegan Garden Board

For a warm summer evening with friends or family, this plant-based board is hard to beat. The flavours are fresh and light, but there are plenty of substantial dishes, so no one will be left feeling hungry. The mix of fresh vegetables adds colour to the board, but there's also plenty of texture to enjoy. From crisp and crunchy roast chickpeas and toasted pitta breads, to silky houmous and juicy, sweet tomatoes. This combination of colours and textures gives this board a lot of visual appeal and makes it fun and interesting to eat, so don't expect to have much in the way of leftovers. Like lots of the vegetable-based boards, this grazing platter is best eaten soon after assembling – especially if you want to enjoy the falafels and chickpeas hot. Have the veggies ready in your fridge and make anything like the houmous ahead. Then start building your board while the falafel and chickpeas cook, so you can call everyone to the table as soon as it's ready.

Serves 6

250g Roast Chickpeas (see overleaf)
300g Houmous (see page 120 or use
    ready-made)
400g broccoli, broken into florets
1 cucumber, sliced
2 long red peppers, halved and sliced
16 falafels
8 pitta breads, toasted
100g black olive tapenade
200g olives, drained
1–2 tbsp olive oil
a pinch of fresh chopped parsley (optional)
100g pretzels
400g cherry tomatoes on the vine
100g brazil nuts
1 pomegranate
25g pea shoots or watercress,
    to garnish
1–2 limes, sliced into wedges, to serve

Make the roast chickpeas following the recipe overleaf. If you're making the houmous, follow the recipe on page 120.

The broccoli florets can be served raw as crudités, but you can also steam them for 1–2 minutes until they're bright green and just starting to soften. This can make them a little easier to eat. If you prefer them steamed, do that first and then let them cool.

Prepare the cucumber and red peppers. Warm the falafels through, following the packet instructions. Toast the pitta breads.

Arrange a few bowls on your grazing board. Spoon the roast chickpeas, houmous, tapenade, and olives into bowls. Drizzle the olive oil on the houmous and add a pinch of chopped parsley, if liked. Place the falafels and toasted pitta breads into bowls or plates and arrange on the board.

Fill in the gaps with the remaining ingredients, tearing open the pomegranate and garnishing the board with pea shoots or watercress. Add a few wedges of lime for squeezing. Serve straight away.

ROAST CHICKPEAS

Serves 4

400-g tin chickpeas
3 tbsp olive oil
sea salt and freshly ground black pepper
1 tsp cumin seeds
1 tsp sumac
1 tsp dried thyme
1 tsp sesame seeds
2–3 fresh flat-leaf parsley sprigs, finely chopped

Preheat the oven to 200°C/Fan 180°C/Gas 6. Drain the chickpeas and tip out onto a few sheets of kitchen paper. Pat dry, then tip onto a baking tray. Drizzle over the olive oil and season with a little salt and pepper.

Roast the chickpeas in the hot oven for 20–25 minutes, taking the tray out to shake it and turn the chickpeas every 10 minutes. When they're ready, the chickpeas should be browned and crispy looking.

While the chickpeas roast, toast the cumin seeds in a dry frying pan for 1–2 minutes until aromatic. Tip into a mixing bowl and add the other spices.

Tip the roasted chickpeas into the bowl with the spices and toss to mix. Add the chopped parsley and toss a few more times to mix in the fresh herbs. Serve the chickpeas warm or cold. The chickpeas are best eaten on the day they're made.

Study Snacks Board

Anyone who has ever faced an all-night study session before an exam, or left it a little late to finish writing their essay (or their book) will know the value of snacks. A good range of snacks will keep you going while you try to cram information into your brain before it's too late. The secret is to have a mix of textures and flavours. This single serve board is loaded with nuts, dried fruit, and cereals, offering a tasty combination of crunchy, smooth, sweet, and salty that will help power you through the long hours of study. It's also a great snack mix to have on hand for long business meetings – simply scale it up for the number of people in the room.

Serves 1

25g peanuts
30g almonds
40g pecans
25g pistachios
15g cashews
30g Honey & Nut Granola (see page 81 or use ready-made)
3 Ritz crackers
15g dried cranberries
40g chocolate-covered raisins
50g popcorn
15g dried mango
25g toasted coconut chips
25g currants
40g mini pretzels
25g breakfast cereal, like Cheerios

If you'd like to add a spice mix to one or all of the nuts, follow the suggestions opposite. If you'd like to make your own granola, use the recipe on page 81.

Arrange all the snacks in a box divided into small sections, or place them in small bowls on a plate. Dip into them as and when you need to.

SPICE MIXES FOR NUTS

Much like Bridget Jones, nuts are perfect just as they are. But that doesn't mean we don't want to spice things up occasionally. These spice mixes will add heat, sugar, and savoury richness to any combination of nuts. They can all be used with approximately 400g nuts, and that can be a mix or your just favourite nut.

Holiday Spice: Combine 1 tablespoon rapeseed oil with 1 teaspoon ground ginger, 1 teaspoon ground cinnamon, and 1 teaspoon ground cardamom. Add to the nuts, spread out on a baking tray and toast for 10 minutes at 160°C/Fan 140°C/Gas 3. Remove from the oven and drizzle over 2 tablespoons honey. Return to the oven for 5 minutes, then cool completely before transferring to a bowl or container.

Sweet & Spicy: Combine 2 tablespoons melted butter with 1 teaspoon cayenne pepper, 1 teaspoon ground cinnamon, 1 teaspoon ground cumin, and ½ teaspoon sea salt. Add to the nuts, spread out on a baking tray and toast for 10 minutes at 160°C/Fan 140°C/Gas 3. Remove from the oven and sprinkle over 2 tablespoons Demerara sugar. Return to the oven for 5 minutes, then cool completely before transferring to a bowl or container.

Super Savoury: Combine 1 tablespoon rapeseed oil with 1 teaspoon dried rosemary, ½ teaspoon garlic granules, ½ teaspoon mustard powder, ½ teaspoon smoked paprika, ½ teaspoon cayenne pepper, and ½ teaspoon sea salt. Add to the nuts, spread out on a baking tray and toast for 15 minutes at 160°C/Fan 140°C/Gas 3. Cool completely before transferring to a bowl or container.

Tropical Fruit Platter

A treat for two, this gorgeous fruit platter would make a beautiful breakfast or afternoon snack for anyone trying to recreate the vibes of their last holiday – or the holiday they're hoping to take. It's a mouthwatering mix of fresh fruits, simply prepared and served. When ingredients are this stunning, they don't need much fussing. Most of these fruits won't oxidize and start to brown straight after cutting, so you have a little bit of time between arranging the platter and serving, but don't leave it too long. You don't want the fruits to start to dry out. A sweet mango lassi served on the side makes this a more substantial snack, so if you're planning on starting the day with this grazing board, then be sure to include the lassi.

Serves 2

1 ripe mango, hedgehogged (see right)
500g watermelon, sliced into wedges
1 papaya, deseeded, peeled, and sliced
1 dragon fruit, sliced
1 large banana, peeled and sliced
1 kiwi fruit, peeled and sliced
1 lime, halved
edible flowers, to garnish
Mango Lassis, to serve (optional, see below)

Prepare all the fruit. Arrange on a serving board or platter and serve straight away, garnished with edible flowers.

Mango Lassis: If you'd like to serve mango lassis alongside this fruit platter, you can make them by combining 250g mango pulp in a blender with 250ml natural yoghurt, 100ml full-fat milk, and ¼ teaspoon ground cardamom. Blitz until smooth, then taste, and add sugar if needed. If the mango lassi is too thick, add 1–2 tablespoons water and blitz again until you get the consistency you want. Serve straight away, over ice if liked.

HOW TO HEDGEHOG A MANGO

Start by slicing the two fat cheeks off the mango, as close to the stone as possible. Use a small, sharp knife to score lines down the inside of these cheeks, slicing into the mango flesh but not all the way through the skin. Try to score these lines evenly apart, around 1 cm between each one.

Now score lines horizontally across the mango cheeks, to create squares. Press your fingers into the back of the mango cheeks, pushing them so they pop out and the squares of mango look like hedgehogs.

Slice the thinner cheeks off the mango stone, slicing as close to the stone as possible. Thinly slice these thinner sections. The mango hedgehogs and slices are ready to serve.

There is normally some mango left on the stone. You can slice this off and dice it, but it tends to look a bit messy. Take these bits as the chef's reward.

Index

Credits

All reasonable efforts have been made by the authors and publishers to trace the copyright owners of the material quoted in this book and of any images reproduced in this book. In the event that the authors or publishers are notified of any mistakes or omissions by copyright owners after publication, the authors and publishers will endeavour to rectify the position accordingly for any subsequent printing.

All listed in alphabetical order

Acknowledgements

The author wishes to thank the friends and family who were willing to be guinea pigs for my recipes, including my mum and dad, my sisters Alex and Cara, the twins Liam and Niamh, and Gill Penlington. I'd also like to thank Jacqui Caulton the designer, Kate Reeves-Brown the copy editor, proofreaders Kathy Steer and Rachel Malig, indexer Vanessa Bird, and picture researchers Shifting Pixels, as well as my editor Sarah Varrow for steering the book so thoughtfully, and everyone involved in its production at HarperCollins.